NEO-ECO-LIBERALISM

CHANGE MONEY,
CHANGE EVERYTHING

K. HALLAGAN

To Sean Broun

1969 - 2020.

I miss the banter.

PREFACE

I first got pulled into a climate protest in the early noughties. Once below the placards what surprised me most, was how sensible and civil it all was. Amongst the throng I was rubbing shoulders with glaciologists, ornithologists, meteorologists – all academics with an environmental edge. Since then I have participated in six or seven more, and each time as the protests swell, it is getting harder to find the scientists, with ordinary people like you and me beginning to comprehend the magnitude of what's at stake. But you'll still find them, the men and women committing their lives to exposing the truth. Whether hunched over a desk, in a lab or on the streets, protesting.

On my first encounter, one explained how he had spent years in the Antarctic examining the receding ice sheets and his immense pride in contributing to research papers published in major scientific journals, only then to feel his entire life's work was being wasted with the governments lack of action.

On the second march, I met a professor who purchased a field deep in the Devonshire countryside – not for profit or pleasure but to prepare for what he termed 'societal breakdown.' Hearing this, I couldn't help but question if he, having spent years researching the data, hadn't been overpowered by it all and took to purchasing the field as a kind of refuge. 'Not my area,' he replied, smiling. 'Bio-chemistry. But I've read enough to know and am hedging my bets.' And anyway, he, like every researcher you meet, was too level-headed.

These scientists have given up believing in the government and democracy. They are preparing. Neither are they alone. In a recent paper intended not for the public or government but the staff and fellow scholars, Professor Jem Bendell had this to say:

> *The approach of the paper is to analyse recent studies on climate change and its implications for our ecosystems, economies and societies, as provided by academic journals and publications direct from research institutes. That synthesis leads to a conclusion there will be a near-term collapse in society with serious ramifications for the lives of readers.*[1]

The lives of readers...' The climate crisis is no longer the exclusive concern of our grandchildren but you and me. These are not isolated viewpoints. Professor Sir David King – former Chief Scientific Advisor to the UK government – stated: 'It's appropriate to be scared. We predicted temperatures would rise, but we didn't foresee these sorts of extreme events we're getting so soon.'

Professor Jo Haigh, Imperial College London, endorsed him: 'David King is right to be scared – I'm scared too.'[2]

These warnings of climate change are hardly new. Scientists first discovered the so-called 'greenhouse effect,' back in 1861.[3] Since then, the alarm bells have been ringing more frequent, and its effect all the more severe.

For many people, the final straw came when the Intergovernmental Panel on Climate Change (IPCC) declared its twelve-year deadline in 2018, only for President Trump not to rescind from claiming it *a hoax,* but retrench that belief by withdrawing from the Paris Climate Agreement.

Slammed between 'we're damned' and 'doing nothing', it is unsurprising why there has been a rise in *enviro*-mental health issues or people taking to the streets demanding change.

Witnessing this shift at grassroots level, many believe the tide is now turning, assisted by the likes of Extinction Rebellion, Greta Thunberg. Yet the protests and our governments lacklustre approach are never going to be enough. What we need is to put the environment at the core of our decisions. These thoughts are not mine nor the scientists on the march, but Patricia Espinosa, the head of the Paris Climate Agreement, referring to the lack of response from nations that signed the Paris accord.

> *'It is incredible to think that just when nations are facing an emergency that could eventually end human life on this planet, many are sticking to their business-as-usual approach… What we need to put on the table is something much more radical and much more transformative than what we have been doing until now.'*

26th February 2021

The purpose of this book is not to distribute doom or despair, but grounded hope.

Recognising how our economy operates against our scientist's warnings, Neo-ECO-liberalism *(NEL)* aim is to reverse this, while reinvigorating our economy by going to the heart of how it functions, *the exchange mechanism.*

Instead of imposing unfair regulations on businesses from above, it redraws the framework on how companies can grow by locking a green incentive into the medium of money itself, providing the opportunity for capitalists and consumers to profit from preventing climate change, correcting what has unto now, been 'history's greatest case of market failure.[4]

CONTENTS

PART 1 – WHERE WE STAND

The Three Crises

PART 2 – THE CAUSES

The Problem with Neoliberalism

PART 3 – THE SOLUTIONS

Neo-ECO-liberalism, the Solution

INTRODUCTION:

ONE VOICE, OUR VOICE!

In the spring of 2012, on the stage at the Edinburgh Science Festival, was stood the NASA physicist, James Hansen. Alongside him sat Lord Giddens, the ex-director of the London School of Economics (LSE) and Professor Pete Smith, contributor to the IPCC,[5] the UN body created to report on climate change and winner of the Nobel Peace Prize in 2007. The title of the lecture was *'Climate Breakdown, our Future.'*

Firing out the facts, one by one, they explained…

'There will be creations of drought-prone regions in North America and Asia,' said Hansen. 'Erosion of ice sheets, rising sea levels. All of these impacts have already happened or are well underway. Global warming increases both extremes of the Earth's water cycle. Heatwaves and droughts on the one hand, directly from the warming, but also because the warmer atmosphere holds more water vapour with its latent energy, rainfall will become more extreme and there will be stronger storms and greater flooding. Yet the governments continue with business as usual, and what's worse is they force the public to subsidise

fossil fuels by $400-500 billion dollars per year worldwide. This path, if continued, guarantees that we will pass the tipping point leading to ice sheet disintegration that will accelerate out of control, the increasing outbreak of floods and droughts will impact upon the breadbaskets of the world, causing massive famines and economic decline.'

Finishing his speech, as James Hansen took to his seat the atmosphere transformed, from a kind of restrained hope to one of tense dread. As if to endorse this feeling, a member of the audience stood and stamped her foot. *'You sit here and talk as if it's over already. Why? None of us want this. We want change!'* Applauded by the crowd as much for her vim and vigour, as well as her words, the panel were taken aback. Not knowing how to respond, they turned their indignation towards the politicians before ending the talk, claiming our best hopes lay not with our governments anymore, but *China!*

Making my way out into the chilled Edinburgh air, something troubled me. Not the bleak vision that had been sown, nor the peculiarity of China taking centre stage, but the contradictory nature of our principles. Why is it that our best hope lay with China when we were a democracy? And if none of us want this, why is so little being done? Something was failing us, but what – democracy, capitalism or ourselves?

PART 1: WHERE WE STAND

THREE CRISES

1. THE END OF HISTORY

An Economic Crisis

In 1989, shortly after the fall of the Berlin Wall, an article titled *'The End of History?'* was published in the American magazine *'The National Interest.'*

Its author, Fukuyama, referred not to the end of history through events per se, but of political ideas. His argument was rooted in a Hegelian/Marxist perspective, where both philosophers saw history as one long socio-political struggle, striving to reach an end-goal. Civilisation, they believed, had not so much advanced through people and culture, but a process of technological achievements. Starting from tribal society, [6] it progressed slowly to subsistence agriculture, from where slavery sprung, before developing into feudalism, followed by the industrial era. After which, according to Marx, communism would then rise.

Fukuyama, however, on witnessing the mass demonstrations against communism and the fall of the Berlin wall, believed it had arrived at a different endpoint than the one prescribed by Marx – liberal democracy coupled with the free market.

He was not without his critics, but since there was not one economic power of force in existence, that wasn't embracing globalisation and the principles of the free market, they had great difficulty putting forward any sensible argument. Neoliberalism, it appeared, had won.

But it was near twenty years later, in 2008, when his theory developed huge cracks. The stock markets had crashed and property prices were crumbling. It was the financial crisis. Banks were now mired in debt and were unable to forward loans to businesses. Consumers too took fright, demanding their money back from the banks.

On the London Stock Exchange, The Royal Bank of Scotland (RBS), the biggest bank in the world at the time,[7] had its share price plummet by 96%. While Lloyds and Barclays crashed 89% and 90% respectively. Northern Rock, a bank that aggressively borrowed to expand their share of domestic mortgages, had people at the door, queuing in long lines down the street – the first run on a UK bank in over a hundred and fifty years.

In New York, Bear Stearns, which employed over 13,000 people and made over $2 billion in profit,[8] failed to keep up its payments and was forced to go cap-in-hand to the Federal Reserve. Nor was it alone. Freddie Mac and Fannie May soon followed, two of the largest mortgage providers in the United States. Then towering even over them came another, Lehman Brothers. This bank had over $600 billion in assets and represented the fourth-largest bank in the US – an institution considered *too big to fail.*

It did.

Up until this point, it was widely believed if any bank were in difficulty, the Federal Reserve would help prop it up.

Not this time.

A cold shiver ran down the spine of the entire financial industry - it was no longer a question of which banks would fall, but when? Merrill Lynch, UBS, RBS and Alliance & Leicester all stood in line, waiting, as did AIG (the world's biggest insurer), Bradford & Bingley, Citigroup and Fortis. Interlaced with these were other banks and businesses through contracts, orders and payment schemes.

The entire financial system that underpinned capitalism itself was on the verge of collapse. Staring this in the face, governments had little choice but to bail out the banks quickly, or face societal meltdown.

Martin Wolf, working for the *Financial Times*, had this to say regarding Bear Stearns:

> *'Remember March 14th 2008: it was the day the dream of global free-market capitalism died. For three decades we have moved towards market-driven financial systems. By its decision to rescue Bear Stearns, the Federal Reserve, the institution responsible for monetary policy in the US chief protagonist of free-market capitalism, declared this era over.'*

Is it?

Accidents Waiting to Happen

The city of Edinburgh has a rich history when it comes to finance and economics. It was the base of the Scottish Enlightenment, preceding continental Europe's by thirty years and the home of Adam Smith[9] when he wrote *The Theory of Moral Sentiments* and *The Wealth of Nations,* widely accepted as *the* foundation of modern economics. The first-ever society of accountants sprouted from within its walls in 1854. Many banks and financial institutions still choose to base their headquarters there.[10] There is even a museum devoted to money proudly perched and overlooking the city's epicentre. But secluded down the dead-end of a back street in an unassuming, squat and end-of-terrace house lies hidden, *'The Library of Mistakes.'*

Few people know about it, even fewer venture in. But if you are lucky enough to find it and enter, you will discover every shelf weighed down with books devoted to the world of finance. There are tomes on banking, essays on economics, and a plethora of articles and papers dedicated to business, politics and human behaviour, all of which is inextricably linked to the markets.

I was privileged to be the library's warden once, though I wonder why, not a soul entered, at least while I was there. Some may boggle why anyone would want to. Who reads such dry, dull subjects on the likes of insurance, economics or banking? But, then again, why do so few when it is money that forces us out of bed and makes us commute, against our will, to a job we may well not want, abhor or even hate. Like it or loathe it, fact is, money governs our daily lives. We dance to it as it dictates, and when the money stops, we all fall down. Money is more than a mere law, it's a transcendental faith.

Yet this little temple is not always empty. Investors, economists and Professors drop in from time to time, searching for that ever-elusive bit of data. Or to come and listen to the talks and lectures, and all confess, despite the financial crisis, little has changed. The financial industry – and capitalism itself – is in dire need of reform. The question is how to go about it.

Take HBOS (Halifax & Bank of Scotland) for instance. It came to represent the biggest corporate failure in British history, and it was a business these sages and seers knew well, for it just so happened to be headquartered in Edinburgh. And all concurred, it was 'an accident waiting to happen.'[11]

First, there was the *Regulatory Failure.*

Banking is big business. In the UK they have balance sheets the size of sovereign governments. They bring in investment, supply a great many jobs and pay tax. Because of which, the UK has a very large regulatory rulebook. However, it is rarely, if ever, enforced simply because the banks don't want to be interfered with and regularly threaten to relocate abroad if the government even so much as discuss imposing regulations, which would give the UK economy a huge knock. The result of which, the government didn't dare touch it.

Second to this, came the *Auditing Failure.*

The task of every auditor is to examine the financial records of a business to ensure they are accurate, transparent and taxes are paid on time. KPMG – one of the 'Big Four'[12] – was solely responsible for the books at HBOS. However, after its collapse the parliamentary enquiry that took place, looking into why it had fallen, discovered huge gaps in the bank's funding and its liquidity revealing clear reckless growth. KPMG had failed to meet the board once to question them, which the enquiry put down to what is commonly termed a 'golden contract.' So-called because winning a deal with a large bank gives you a great deal of *bolt on benefits,* through contracts such as commercial law applications and insolvencies, which were not just paid for by the bank but enforced by them upon their clients. As such, just like the example above, being too firm with the bank, is effectively biting the hand that feeds you.

Then there was the *Corporate Governance Failure.*

The head of regulatory risk at HBOS was Paul Moore, whose job was to warn the board of the bank when they were crossing a line and becoming too complacent in their drive for growth. Records show he repeatedly challenged the board on these grounds, as it risked the long-term integrity of the bank's security. In response to raising his concerns, rather than heed his advice, the board had him sacked!

And last of all came the *Failure of the Boardroom,* which is particularly worth noting, for it is here, where the ideas spring and the decisions are made that mould not just companies, but much of our society and culture, and which is failing to address the one issue which it should be helping to alleviate, not aggravate.

There were four individuals on the board. The first, James Crosby, was the mastermind behind the Halifax/Bank of Scotland merger that formed HBOS. He was said to have a detailed grasp of financial risk. Yet no sooner had the merger been sealed, when he put in place an aggressive financial formula. Wanting to raise the corporation's value quickly, he employed a combination of high-risk strategies and deception, using equity stakes in businesses and corporate vehicles through a lending process, to make the equity and debt become blurred. The purpose of which was simply to enable HBOS to lend even more (going against Paul Moore's advice). The board then pursued a policy to promote share buybacks and raised the dividend pay-out of HBOS year-on-year, which indicated vast profits while deliberately hiding the risks, loose controls and monitoring. Playing to the market like this proved highly lucrative, as more investors jumped on board. In 2001 the HBOS balance sheet stood at £275 billion, and by 2008 it had swollen to £631 billion – the year it all came crashing down. James Crosby however, left before that, to join as Deputy, of all places, The Financial Services Authority, making him immune to blame; or until Paul Moore spoke up, for as soon as the Parliamentary Enquiry learnt this, Crosby stepped down.

Behind him was Andy Hornby, a man who had zero banking experience. Crosby had enlisted him on account of his academic record. Graduating from Harvard with an MBA, he came the top of his class, numbering eight-hundred students. According to the parliamentary enquiry, on taking over from Crosby as CEO, he ignored all warnings to continue an expansionist policy, with the sole aim of getting an ever-larger share of the domestic market.

Lord Stevenson was another colleague with relatively little experience in banking. His lack of knowledge led to poor corporate governance as he had failed to hold the senior staff to account. At the time of the enquiry, he said the reckless lending wasn't his fault as he was only there part-time – he happened to earn £815,000 a year, *part-time.*

The last of the four was Peter Cummings who had worked his way up within the Bank of Scotland. The board had been particularly impressed with the returns he had made in expanding the corporate loan book. Given his impressive figures, Lord Stevenson cut loose his reins, effectively giving him an open chequebook to buy into any businesses he saw fit. Even as late as February 2008, when the financial crisis was already unfolding, Cummings was quoted as saying: *'Some people look as if they're losing their nerve, beginning to panic even in today's testing property environment, not us.'* One month later, shares in HBOS fell off a cliff.

All board members broke the No1 rule of banking: to provide a safe and secure haven for people's savings. Why they failed was because their policies served the financial markets and their own selfish ambition. But what's most interesting in what happened at HBOS, is it not a one-off example in banking failure or even the financial crisis, it is down to how capitalism itself is structured, as it's a system directly focused around the exchange-value i.e., not geared towards improving the needs of individuals or that of society, but towards growth and profit making businesses work without a purpose, for which there are many ways to achieve this.

Take the model many capitalists like to promote - how competition forces businesses to improve their product. Why in today's globalised market, should business labour at this when it's much more lucrative to market your product heavily, evade tax, move the factory abroad or lobby government? These methods certainly raise earnings or the share price, but does it improve society? Or why not go the exact opposite way and engage in planned obsolescence? After all, designing your product to falter or fall apart only encourages consumers to consume, yet more, leading to greater growth. Doesn't Adam Smith's theory also claim that increased competition will drive down prices so consumers can buy more?

Take *Nike*. Their sneakers can retail at near the $190 mark, yet in reality cost around $20 to make.[13] This, from the same corporation that chooses to *reinvest* $3 billion of its $27.8 billion revenue through 'demand creation', using the likes of celebrity endorsements to bombard us with irrational beliefs that their product is *the best* and will make you a champion in your field – not training, tuition or discipline of course, but *Nike*.

Our business culture is so geared towards growth that it has became society's *raison d'etre*. Adam Smith wrote: 'that it is not for benevolence that we go to work each day, but for our own selfish ambition.' His observations were as clear then as they are now. But to what length?

When a company grows in a *mature* marketplace, it erodes the market share of other companies which could be serving both the individual and society better? Where is the pivot that decides this? Inside the mind of the consumer of course, which business cleverly manipulates and deliberately deceives. Was HBOS a better financial institution than RBS, and RBS better than Lloyds or Nationwide? No. HBOS grew faster on account of its deception and deceit – blurring the gap between equity and debt while ramping up the advertising and taking bolder risks with *other people's money!* That was all. Ultimately, the members of the board saw a loophole in the public's and investor's ignorance and designed stratagems to tap this.

This practice, along with others mentioned, exposes how the current rules have enabled business to abuse their position in the market, making capitalism become derailed from its central tenet – to fulfil people's needs – feeding discord between the three main parties (The Public, Government & Business). This wayward shift in the economy, from serving society as a whole to favouring those rich with assets,[14] reveal how the fruits of our economy are no longer trickling down,[15] as the rich squirrel funds from the real economy into tax-free havens, causing funding to shrink which siphons the very lifeblood from what progress demands – investment in innovation.

Now contrast that with Rousseau's quote three centuries past, at the time of the Enlightenment:

'Man acquires with civil society, moral freedom, which alone makes man the master of himself; for to be governed by appetite alone is slavery, while obedience to a law one prescribes to oneself is freedom.'

This begs the question, what law do we adhere to in this day and age if not appetite, given the goal of every government[16] is near-fixated on GDP, and every business directed on growth and higher sales while ignoring their purpose to serve society. Moreover, if every nation were to achieve a growth rate of just 3% per annum, in little under a quarter of a century, humanity's global consumption would double. What do we mine, cut down or throw our waste onto then? How did we ever come to this, and more importantly, why hasn't our economy evolved to recognise the limits of what scientists deem safe? It is as if the only vision we are capable of today, is growth!

With HBOS, not only was the board given free rein to pursue its own selfish ambition, but even the auditors and the government itself. Further still, no one was made accountable. Least of all the executives. For on being found guilty by the parliamentary enquiry, not one member was properly penalised, let alone jailed. Our trust, belief and sense of shared values are being eroded - the three pillars on which every society depends.

As a consequence, now the public are angry. Angry at corporations who reward board members huge bonuses; Angry at globalisation for taking their jobs, and most of all, angry at the politicians who pander to business over them. And now the financial crisis has spread into that of politics.

2. THE DISENCHANTED

A Political Crisis

Imagine you were a nurse working for the NHS[17] when the pandemic struck and your hospital comes under increasing strain. Overwhelmed by the ill and suffering, unable to say no, knowing you hold in your hands the difference between life and death, you work the extra nights, despite knowing you are putting your own life at risks. Long exhaustive days pass into months pass, only then to discover, that for all the extra hours and days you sacrifice, your government rewards you with a paltry pay rise of 1%. Equivalent to 'a kick in the teeth.'[18]

Knowing what you and your colleagues went through, feeling undervalued, imagine what it then feels like to hear that one of the big pharmaceutical corporations has been caught - red-handed - pumping up their prices purely to capitalise at the expense of the NHS,[19] while their CEO receives a pay packet of $17 million,[20] not for innovation or efficiency focused on bettering the world, but exploiting the vulnerable and you!

Or say you were a student about to graduate under a mountain of debt, when you read your Vice-Chancellor was paid the sum of £468,000.[21]

What if you are a mother watching over your children play, knowing the world they will inherit will be one bleaker and more dangerous, never giving them the quality of life, you had.

Or say are one of the unlucky, having stood in the path of hurricane Harvey, Irma or Katrina, only to witness your President, the 'Leader of the Free World' declare climate change '...*a hoax? I mean, it's a money-making industry, ok?*[22] This, despite over 99%[23] of Scientists declaring climate change real, happening and an existential threat.

Or imagine yourself a Mr X, the proud owner of a high street shop. One night you hear a shout from outside your window. Looking out, you see you worse nightmare has returned - again! Venturing downstairs, you wade through the knee-deep and murky water to find your stock completely ruined. This is not the second or even third time this has happened, but the sixth! Nor is it caused by a freak storm but a leak from the watermains that *Thames Water* is responsible for maintaining, yet takes no responsibility for. What's more, this is a public utility the government sold which now happens to be owned by a consortium of firms from Kuwait, China, Canada and the United Arab Emirates who have connection to the area, other than making money of course.

Neither does this nightmare stop. For imagine, one month after the clean-up, you pay your water bill and take a seat to relax and pick-up the newspaper to read: *Thames Water cannot be taken at face value for anything it says*'[24] What's more, it's responsible for spewing 1.4 billion litres of raw sewerage over two years into the River Thames (its very namesake) at a time when, due to the effects of climate change and the rising population, the demand for water in the UK will well exceed supply in twenty years – especially in the south, where Thames Water holds the contract for maintaining much of the infrastructure.

Perhaps you think this *true story* of the shopkeeper a little extreme given how he is particularly hard done by? But then what of the other fifteen million customers of Thames Water, representing around a quarter of the entire UK population? Research by the University of Greenwich found its customers are now paying around £2.3 billion more, each year, for water and sewerage, then when the utility was state-owned. So, where does so much of this extra money go? Not to improve the quality or efficiency of the infrastructure, but to the shareholders in the form of dividends and bonuses; to the board members whose pay has soared while the company uploads itself with debt in order to pay the minimum of tax.[25] If you still happen to not feel anything wrong with how Thames Water operates, then I suspect you would be in a tiny minority, as these policies go against basic human values.

So, the upshot of the banking crisis is nothing has really changed. The banking regulations may have tightened a little and the economy put back on track,[26] but ultimately, what happened at Thames Water is no different than what happened at HBOS. Stories such as these are not rare or isolated incidents. Companies worldwide employ the same financial models taught through MBAs at business schools – be it Harvard or Singapore, Mumbai or Oxford – how to beat your competition and increase profit and growth.

Blinkered from our values, this mantra is in itself crude, yet when mixed with the reckless culture of the boardroom, it goes beyond this, as it feeds an economy that fails miserably on the biggest crisis we have ever yet faced, *climate breakdown*.

3. THERE'S NO GOING BACK

The Planetary Crisis

'For me, the really concerning aspect of this is that now, more than at any time in our history, our species needs to work together. We face awesome environmental challenges: climate breakdown, food production, overpopulation, the decimation of other species, epidemic disease, acidification of the oceans. Together, they are a reminder that we are at the most dangerous moment in the development of humanity. We now have the technology to destroy the planet on which we live, but have not yet developed the ability to escape it.'

Stephen Hawking[27]

The more you stare into the face of climate change and ecological breakdown, the more you want to look away. Yet this 'green fatigue' or the facts that feed it, are impossible to ignore, which combined, lay bare the existential angst we are at – denialism or nihilism, take your pick. Some choose to read the data and become enraged or descend into depression. While others choose to turn away, seeing it all too scary. Read it or leave it? It's your choice. Only problem is, as the scientists mentioned the gap is narrowing and soon there may be no choice. Adapt now, or die.

Since records began in 1850, nineteen of the twenty hottest years have occurred since 2000, the only exception being 1998. In 2003 a heatwave in Europe took 70,000 lives in a matter of days. France, Germany, Poland and the Czech Republic all broke their highest summer temperatures in 2019; Alaska one week later.[28] According to analysts at the BBC, the world experiences twice as many days over 50°C then in the 1980's.[29] Yet, it is said, the maximum temperature that the human body can tolerate under sustained conditions is 42.3°C.[30]

The number of extreme storms has doubled since the 1980's.[31]

California struggled to recover from its worst drought in 1200 years only to have another shortly after. While the UK recently suffered its wettest ever December (which is saying something).

Wildfires have ignited from the Arctic to the Amazon with ever increasing length and fury. The world's glaciers melt as our scientists let loose the sirens with yet more warnings, telling coastal planners to *'brace themselves.'*[32]

In Germany, the oldest continuous records on monitoring insects exists, and in a 2017 study, it announced a 75% fall in insect biomass over the last twenty-seven years.[33] What was more shocking than the numbers, was this data wasn't gathered from or adjacent to farms that practice intensive monoculture, nor near industrial zones or even suburbs, but buried within nature reserves. It doesn't stop. For neither are they plummeting in just developed nations, but some of the remotest parts on Earth - Puerto Rico, deep in a distant part of the jungle. Researchers there discovered insect numbers had been eradicated by 89% over a thirty-six-year period.[34] This collapse has huge ramifications along every link further up the food chain.

Meanwhile, the fish in our oceans are on the verge of collapse.[35]

At the same time, every year, we continue to strip the earth of over 90 billion tonnes of its raw natural resources [36] while dumping 2 billion tonnes of our own waste,[37] pushing species of animals and plants in their millions to the brink of extinction.[38] Worse still, 99% of the stuff we throwaway was purchased less than six months ago!

If these warnings are not enough, our oceans swell and their corals bleach[39] and now, the very soil we till and grow our crops in have deteriorated to the point where the nutritional value is half that of what our grandparents had, in their diets.[40]

Despite all of this and more, much more, we continue on the same economic course, so long as it delivers a *healthy profit*.

But making that profit is not going to be so easy to come by soon.

'The economic losses from natural disasters increased eightfold from the sixties to the nineties. About 80% of this resulted from extreme weather-related events. The company now predicts that by 2065, the cost of damages will outstrip the supply of global assets.'[41]

Munich Re, German insurers.

'With continued growth in emissions at historic rates, annual losses in some economic sectors are projected to reach hundreds of billions of dollars by the end of the century — more than the current gross domestic product (GDP) of many US states.[42]'

Fourth National Climate Assessment Vol.II

These two reports – one from the business sector, the other scientific – both acknowledge we are heading to a point where capitalism will soon be unable to function.[43]

Is there any wonder why only 50% of modern-day Americans have faith in capitalism?[44] A mere 19% call themselves capitalists, while 51% of Americans aged between eighteen to twenty-nine don't even support it.[45]

Meanwhile, on the other side of the pond, almost 70% of adults in the UK distrust advertising while 40% don't trust brands.[46]

In fact, all around the world capitalism is being frowned upon as people become more and more disenchanted. In Brazil 57% believe it does more harm than good in its current form. While in the Netherlands that figure is 59%; France 69% and Thailand and India over 75%.[47]

So with scientists 'scared' by global warming; politicians 'concerned' and the public as good as demanding 'change', why aren't we?

The dilemma has not so much been about *changing*, as we all recognise its faults, but change to what exactly?

'It is easier to imagine the end of the world than the end of capitalism.'

Frederic Jameson

While the majority of us are more than willing to sacrifice parts of our lifestyle, only a small number are prepared to make the changes necessary to avert any of the tipping points.[48]

Moreover, if a single state, say France, were to reduce its carbon footprint to zero - representing just 0.87% of the global population - the return on its investment will not go far while the rest of the world continues to dance to the tune of money, reaping those short-term rewards. What's needed is a paradigm shift and one we can all believe in.

Yet if we are to be bold enough to change, it is only prudent to understand what we are changing from, how we got here and what we might well lose.

PART 2:
THE CAUSES

THE PROBLEM

WITH

NEOLIBERALISM

4. OUR MISPLACED FAITH IN PRICES

How Corporations Seized Control

The 1930s echoed similar themes to those played out in the financial crash, only these were troubling times the world over and much worse. The ghost of fascism was already alive and many economies were sunk deep in a recession. None worse than the United States.

Wall Street had collapsed, bringing down with it a slew of banks and the public took to withdrawing money *en masse*. With next to no credit, banks were unable to lend to businesses or invest, causing companies to fold, creating unemployment on a mass scale. This is why it will always be known as, *The Great Depression*.

Many began to question the values of liberalism on witnessing capitalism's failure to deliver. While economists at the time blamed workers for remonstrating, claiming they were demanding too high wages alongside better working conditions. But two economists didn't see it like that. Both were based in London. Both were at the city's School of Economics (LSE) and both had completely contradictory views.

The more senior of the two went by the name of John Maynard Keynes. Instead of seeing it from a neoclassical [49] perspective – the overriding trend at the time – he knew businesses were losing confidence day by day and the only way to restore that was to get the government to kick-start the economy. This required injecting capital into the economy through building new infrastructure – roads, bridges and power stations. Not only would this directly create jobs, but crucially boost business confidence which would encourage people to spend which the state could recoup later by raising taxes.

Frederick Von Hayek believed in no such thing.

A utilitarian entrenched in the beliefs of John Stuart Mill and Adam Smith, to him the state should never interfere unless to *protect the market*. He believed the downward swing in the economy was an organic process. As such, it should be free to organically grow and contract. Then, granted time, it would climb out of the recession on its own accord.

Furthermore, interfering in an economy sends you down a slippery slope towards funnelling power into the hands of dictators – something Hayek was only too aware of, having witnessed the rise of fascism closer to home in his native Austria.

But it was *Keynesian economics* that became the model of choice in the major economies of The West, and Hayek, along with his theory, faded way into the background.

Or that was until 1975, when legend has it that a certain Margaret Thatcher, on taking over leadership of the Conservative party, slammed his book: 'The Constitution of Liberty' across her desk. Now the whole world dances to a different tune, his tune, *Neoliberalism.*

Hayek's eureka moment came when he was observing people at work in the city…

Going to collect his suit he was unexpectedly kept waiting as the tailor was busily occupied calculating the costs of the cloth, buttons and thread, along with the hours it took to sew. He thought little of it until on his way back home, stopping to buy bread, he noticed the baker doing the same thing, only with the sacks of flour and bags of yeast coming into the shop off the lorry. It then dawned on Hayek how the market, powered and steered by individuals, worked far more efficiently than any state institution could ever do, and for a state to interfere and try to correct the market (which Keynes believed) was just sheer folly. The state had not the capability to know, let alone supply the needs and whims of the public at any given moment. Only one thing could: the 'automatic mechanism of adjustment' built into the *point of exchange*. Only *it* recognised the decision of both parties partaking in the exchange through the price, for it recognised the relative scarcity of a product; along with what a vendor hopes to gain above the labour/material costs they've invested; and the expense a consumer is willing to pay for the relative satisfaction they believe they will gain in purchasing the goods. This makes the entire economy gravitate towards this flux point, and as such it acts as *the scales* of where all needs and utility – or *value* – were weighed for society.

This faith in the exchange, or marketplace, bolts 'neo' onto 'liberalism', for classic liberalism was based upon *laissez-faire* economics that believes business should be left alone to do its job, while the state should be left alone to do its. Whereas under neoliberalism, the sole role of the state was neither to leave the market alone nor to interfere, but *serve it*. In other words, fine-tune and maintain the perfect environment by advancing an institutional framework for the competitive forces of the market to fight it out on society's behalf.

And it is this belief in the exchange mechanism where the crux of the problem lies. Having *blind faith* in a price fails to account what we're really buying into, as it hardly grasps the wider repercussions of society's ills.

When taking a wander down to your local store, you'll find goods from Battersea to Bombay, Zanzibar to New Zealand. Or browse through the window of any clothes store where you can choose the correct attire for your chosen activity or how best you want to express yourself: colour, style, comfort or attitude. Then when back home, *click and* have a hot pizza designed around your allergy delivered right to your door. Then *click* on your latest TV which coolly curves and sit back to watch a story unfold tailored perfectly to your mood. Then when it's finished, take your life-extending medicine before booking a ticket to anywhere in the world, or out into *space!*[50]

Yet as wondrous as all of these are, each serves to solve one single problem, whereas climate change is not. It is a global issue that affects all of us, as we affect it and as such, it's far too complex for any individual or business to assimilate, let alone process and solve. Thus, instead of helping us to grasp this thorny issue, the market encourages us to ignore it through buying thoughtlessly instead, and as such it slams the door shut on what is all of our collective responsibility.

For example, does a wheat farmer factor into his profit/loss analysis the issue of soil erosion? Or does a shoe manufacturer comprehend the deforestation when purchasing leather soles over rubber, or PVC over bio-fabricated ones?

What of a café – do they understand the issue of waste and use compostable coffee cups as opposed non-recyclable ones? The list goes on and on and on. But if millions of businesses fail to take issues like this into account, what of the billions of consumers?

5. THE MAZE OF THE MARKET

The Blind Consumer

Picture a mother taking her child shopping. The child sees some cheese or a chocolate bar with a smiley cow on the wrapper and wants it. Not for the flavour of course, nor its nutritional value but because the child's imagination associates the product with being happy, just as a teenager does a sports car for sexual appeal or an adult eying up another's shoes for prestige.

What does the mother do? Faced with the decision she - like everybody - wants to make the right choice. But what exactly is *the right choice*? To make the child happy or to do what is right for the child in her wisdom? Fulfilling the child's desire solves a short-term issue, but what about the long-term? How healthy is it? Is the company reputable? What is the financial burden to her?

Rushed as we are in this busy world, odds are she makes a snap decision based upon price, time, familiarity and the child's present emotional state, thereby sidestepping her rational, long-term concerns altogether. Thus avoiding 'what's *really* best' for the child. But could she not have got more for her money? Where does the money she part with go? Is the company playing its part in the community and helping her child's future foundations?

If you were to inform her better about the consequences of her decision, results have repeatedly proved she would – as we all would – take due consideration. But with the information not easily accessible she was indirectly distracted with what is effectively a fallacy instead, stimulating a more basic desire.

From this, it is safe to assume that (a) not only are we fickle – our feelings steering our thoughts and decisions but (b) due to advertising consistently bombarding us with what are subliminal messages, targeting our most basic and immediate desires (what Plato termed our animal-side), we have become further distracted from pursuing 'what's best' based upon our beliefs and values.[51]

Socrates said the point of a decision is to do what we think is best. Yet (a) not only is this difficult to achieve – best for who and at what price? But often it becomes too hard to analyse every motive and lasting effect and, even if we are fortunate to come to what is a sound decision, (b) results show we rarely stick to it. Plato added to this, saying the soul is divided into three parts: the rational side – when we think what is valuable and good; the animal side – our physical appetite for food, drink or basic desires: and the spiritual – our emotions like anger and so forth. The result is we have a divided soul forever in conflict i.e., business knows what is right but fearing competition does the opposite. Politicians seek virtue but are overcome by their desire for re-election, leaving virtue at the wayside.

Whether a politician, businessman or citizen, this inner friction in our thoughts and decision process appears to be the cause of so many problems, as there is no clear path. However, it is the rational side of the public we need to focus on, as it is the duty of the other two parties to serve them in a democracy, not vice-versa.

In 1762, Rousseau published the *Social Contract*, in which was written:

> *'The passing from the site of nature to the civil society produces a remarkable change in man; it puts justice as a rule of conduct in the place of instinct, and gives his actions the moral quality they previously lacked. It is only then, when the voice of duty has taken the place of physical impulse, and right that of desire, that man, who hitherto thought only of himself, finds himself compelled to act on other principles, and to consult his reason rather than study his inclinations.'*

And in 1929, Freud wrote:

> *'...it is impossible to overlook the extent to which civilisation is built upon a renunciation of instinct, how much it presupposes precisely the non-satisfaction of powerful instincts. This 'cultural frustration' dominates the large field of social relationships between human beings.'*

> Civilisation and Its Discontents.

Absorbing these snippets of wisdom, one can't help but reflect how corporations have become aggressive, focusing the bulk of their efforts on engaging with our instinctual nature – the *anima* – while less effort is spent trying to incentivise us through our rational side, counter to what the leading thinkers of the Enlightenment encouraged us to do.

Just switch on the TV, and you will get to witness some of the results of a business's labour. But to better appreciate the immense effort they undertake at the design stage, just step into the library of your nearest university. There, in the business school department, you will witness what a business expects of their future 'captains of industry.'[52] Books are devoted to the psychology of colours – how each colour can attract or detract; words – how they have the power to encourage or discourage; shapes – how they can express curiosity or disdain; fonts – to denote intelligence, elegance or attitude, to entice specific age groups, cultures or gender. Today, an average young person growing up in the United States experiences 13 000 - 30 000 advertisements on television each year. Furthermore, these figures don't include the likes of marketing content online, in print or at the cinema, billboards on the street, video games or in school. Nor have I mentioned the methods social media giants go to - examining everything we look at, our mouse hovers over, what we click on or buy.

Today advertising has become so invasive that it numbs its supposed effect, as companies jostle and joust to stand out, making it hard to tell one from another. Yet considering its power to leverage sales at a fraction of the cost of designing and producing an improved product, why a business pursues such paths is of no surprise, as it can make the difference between the life and death of a company.

But to repeat, we must ask ourselves as a society, what makes one company more deserved than another? Certainly not advertising, as it hardly benefits society. In fact, advertising detracts from what sells capitalism, *progress!*

> *They say that if you build a better mousetrap than your neighbour, people are going to come running. They are like hell! It's marketing that makes the difference.*
>
> Ed Johnson

Besides, trying to choose the right product is hard enough, without being subjected to dazzling displays, candy-coloured facades and gizmos. Advertising constitutes what is an attack on our psychological sovereignty, crushing what brings out the best in us, which Freud and Rousseau highlighted.

Secondly, given it is immoral to deliberately deceive should we not be overturning this part of our mainstream culture and replacing it with reason instead?

Fort thirdly, numerous studies show it is damaging to our mental health.[53]

And fourthly, it generates excessive waste and energy at a time when it needs drastically to be curbed.[54]

Therefore, would it not be preferable to nudge companies towards investing their energy, time and money into building better products to improve our lives and the world around us, as opposed to serving growth for growth's sake?

In addition to these two obstacles (innately being fickle & overcoming the fallacy of advertising), there is yet another pitfall to overcome, *globalisation.*

Way back, when we existed within micro-communities, our actions were all the more predictable as it was hard not to ascertain their consequences. We knew, for example, not to chop down the apple tree for firewood to keep warm over winter – if we did, the ramifications would be felt the following harvest.

Today, it is nigh impossible to be aware of the corollaries of our decisions. How can we be responsible for the choices we take when they have vanished by distance and time?

In the mother and child scenario, if we were to follow the thread back to the manufacturer, the very opposite could be true of the image portrayed. The premises that produces it has much less probability of being a farm nestled in an alpine meadow of cows, as depicted on the wrapper, and more an industrial facility that happens to import powdered milk & palm oil in its making of processed cheese. It could be owned by a hedge-fund based in the Cayman Islands that has never invested in improving production or ever paid its fair share of tax but uses the business as a cash cow.[55]

The sheer volume of information required to absorb then process the data to come close to the truth (let alone the right decision) confounds us, causing us to shy away, and it is this which conveniently gifts business *a veil* to hide behind, effectively capitalising upon our ignorance.

> *'Unless we deliberately restrict our choices by creating restrictive rules, thereby simplifying the environment that we have to deal with, our bounded rationality cannot cope with the complexity of the world. It is not because the government necessarily knows better that we need regulations. It is in the humble recognition of our limited mental capability that we do.'*
>
> Ha-Joon Chang, Professor of Economics at the University of Cambridge.

Yet the hard fact is, the responsibility lies squarely with us as the consumer is undoubtedly king, as it is we who wield the greatest power as the end-user. Hence, it is our fundamental right and responsibility to know what harm we are inflicting when we purchase something. Without this premise, we are not a society of enlightened citizens, but consumers with our noses in the trough whose *blind choices* are destroying this planet upon which all depend, as power is disproportionately held in the hands of the boardroom who pursue growth and profit at all costs.

Therefore, to survive the coming century, we are left a stark choice. To either:

(a) Abandon neoliberalism altogether by having the state radically restrain the markets and much of our lifestyle in the process; or

(b) Overhaul Hayek's giant number cruncher so it factors society's broader issues into those artificial numbers that make up the price at the point of exchange.

The Invisible Hand
Made Visible

A cluster of institutions have already started to take on the challenge by informing consumers better; 'The Higg Index,' being one, 'The Energy Star' another. Then there is the International Organisation for Standardisation (ISO), Fairtrade, the Rainforest Alliance and the Ellen MacArthur Foundation, to name a few. All of these go some way to inform us, helping to gnaw away at our ignorance. But there is one that stands head and shoulders above the rest, and its success comes down to two factors.

Firstly, the system is mandatory to all manufacturers it applies to.

Secondly, unlike having a basic benchmark of excellence, it utilises capitalism's greatest forte – *competition* – encouraging corporations to vie against one another along the single channel of energy efficiency.

Created for the EU, it is called the 'European Energy Label'. In its most basic sense, it's just a label. But that label displays how efficient the product is when purchasing compared to other models on the market. It exhibits this through the colours and the letters from 'G' to 'A+++'[56], making it both easy and efficient for consumers to absorb.

The rating indicates how much energy the model uses, giving a strong impression of the long-term costs and environmental damage that will be inflicted after the transaction, enabling consumers to peer past the veil business has long exploited.

Further still, because all manufacturers of such products are legally obliged to exhibit the label, it doesn't so much as nudge but pushes business to innovate ever more efficient designs, thus redirecting investment away from industries that are less beneficial for society, like speculation or advertising for example.[57] And for the products that remain inefficient, it gives manufacturers three years notice that there will be a new mandatory minimum standard, or a phasing out of such products (G in this case).

With lighting for example, in swapping incandescent lightbulbs to LED, the average house in the UK used 720 kw hours a year. Today, that figure is down at about 400 kw hours.[58]

Its success was so effective at curbing energy consumption it has since been rolled out to other domestic appliances – washing machines, tumble dryers, vacuums, dishwashers, hairdryers, ovens, heaters, air-conditioning units, as well as lightbulbs, cars and even real estate.

The EU calculated between 1994 and 2020, the energy label saved around 175 Mtoe (million tonnes of oil equivalent) – roughly equal to Italy's entire energy consumption for a year, or 9% of the EU's total energy consumption and a potential 7% reduction in carbon emissions. Or, if looked at financially, it generated a total €55 billion in savings for the European Union, which is equivalent to €465 off every household energy bill.[59]

This saving is projected to grow to 15% of the EU's total energy consumption and 11% of its total carbon emissions by 2030.

Not only does this keep fossil fuels in the ground but lessens the EU's dependency on oil & gas-producing nations.[60]

It is truly remarkable how one such policy - a label - helped so much to lift the veil, enabling the public to see past the dazzling colours, displays and sale signs, giving them a far more honest picture of what they are both buying and saving.

Yet more astonishing, is why it has never been rolled out the world over, given our predicament.[61]

If we were to apply a sustainability label to all goods and services, individuals could make considerable headway on tackling climate change, given its efficiency and transparency at informing consumers, whilst encouraging companies to lean more towards investing in *our needs*, not the boardrooms.

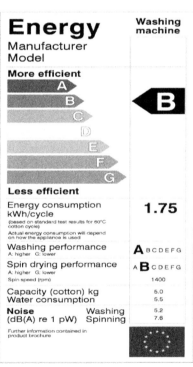

Such a system embraces the principles of neoliberalism well, for although it interjects with the market, it equally enables the state to further retreat from interfering in the economy at the latter stage, the financial clean-up, thus merging both business and public closer, promoting greater *civic engagement* and *trust*. Failing to pursue such policies has given neoliberalism an undeserved reputation. Furthermore, given the lack of vision and political will by successive governments, even if leaders the world over were to suddenly jump on the bandwagon, it would never go far enough to halt climate change alone. Therefore, let us turn away from the consumer's dilemma and return to the conflict of interest business faces between 'doing good' and 'good business,' as highlighted by HBOS and Thames Water.'

Take Lobsters

The conflict of interest for capitalists is hardly new. Plato, in the fourth century BC, wrote:

> *'The more men think of making a fortune, the less they think of virtue, for when riches and virtue are placed together in the scales of the balance, the one always rises as the other always falls.'*

Adam Smith took a different perspective through his 'invisible hand', believing it was only through competition that the selfishness of entrepreneurs can bring about lower prices and innovation, thus advancing society in the process.

Both can be right or wrong under the current structure, for it is widely dependent upon the character of the corporation customarily carved out behind the walls of the boardroom.

However, due to the march of globalisation opening ever-new markets, the escalation in competition squeezes corporations to not just lower their prices but standards too. This law of the jungle is not one of morality or design, but appetite – to sell more and profit more, no matter what. Further to this, having had this seep into our culture for so long, it has come to define success not on virtue or meritocratic grounds, but by how much you have and how quickly you got it!

There is a company located on the west coast of Scotland that trades in lobsters. Caught out at sea, they are brought back to port, loaded onto a truck and transported one hundred miles away to Glasgow airport. Six-thousand miles later, having flown to Bangkok, they are off-loaded with heavy machinery onto an open truck with huge blocks of melting ice. From there, they are transported 180 miles away under the scorching sun to Trat, a town close to the Cambodian border. Here, the lobsters are prepared and packaged by Cambodian immigrants for fifty cents an hour before being returned to the truck. Driven back to the airport, they are put on a plane where they are flown to restaurants in London, Paris[62] and New York. Why? Because even after factoring in the costs for flying thousands of miles, the fifty cents an hour labour costs are a lot cheaper than the minimum wage in the UK.[63]

Burberry, the upmarket fashion brand, destroyed clothes, accessories and perfume valued at £28.6m in 2017 in order to defend its luxury image. Even considering the brand's high prices, that's equal to more than 20,000 of the company's signature trench coats. Neither is this a one-off. The figure was £90 million for the five years before. Nor is it restricted to them but a trend rutted deep into the upper end of the fashion industry. Richemont, which owns the Cartier and Montblanc brands, has bought back €480m worth of watches over the last two years. Maria Malone, principal lecturer on the fashion business course at Manchester Metropolitan University, said: 'Destroying unwanted products is part of that process. The reasoning is they do not want the market flooded with discounts.' Tim Jackson, director of the British School of Fashion, said: 'There's no way they are ever going to solve this problem.'[64]

Or take helium. Despite being the second most common element in the universe, it is relatively scarce here on earth. Its benefits are needed for the use of MRI scanners to cool their super-conductive coils; at CERN, one of the forefronts of science; and to assist babies and deep-sea divers breathing. Yet for all its importance in saving lives and its necessity in research, we happily use it to inflate balloons at kids' parties![65] Helping the price to rise by over 135% in a year.[66]

Here's another. There's a company that boasts proudly to 'Build Ingenuity.' Buying goods from suppliers in the UK, it sends them to the US, only then to have them returned immediately on touching US soil without ever reaching the US market. This takes these unopened boxes on a 7,000–mile jaunt. So why? To save paying tax! When asked what the commercial purpose of sending goods on a circular journey via the US might be, the company said: 'Its delivery process prioritises speed of order and customer service.'[67] This is classic *double-speak*[68] and a very poor one.

Or let's take a bigger brand – Starbucks. Despite the UK being its biggest market outside the US, up until 2013 it made in excess of £3 billion, yet reported taxable profits just once in 15 years! A total of £8.6 million was all it paid to the UK tax office during its first fourteen years in the UK.[69]

Starbucks is not alone. Facebook, Google, Apple are some of the other big brands actively avoiding tax when and where and however they can. Apple itself has been known to harbour $200 billion in offshore accounts to avoid paying US tax. This, the biggest company in the world as I write.

The level of subterfuge a multinational company goes to is extraordinary. A study by the New Economics Foundation in the UK, calculated that for every £1 of value a tax planner contributes to the British economy, £37 is taken out, revealing just how clever and determined corporations are in snooping out loopholes. Would it not be more sensible to have these brain wizards engage their brains in saving the world, rather than saving money!?

These examples further highlight the backwardness of our economy and the sheer distance a business will go to in order to make a buck. Yet we must give them some leeway, as this is not an entirely new phenomenon.

> *To prevent war material reaching the enemy is common sense, but to sell in the highest market is a business duty. Right at the end of August 1939 the British dealers were tumbling over one another in their eagerness to sell Germany tin, rubber, copper and shellac – and this in the clear, certain knowledge that war was going to break out in a week or two. It was about as sensible as selling somebody a razor to cut your throat with. But it was 'good business.'*
>
> George Orwell, 1946. 'Why I write.'

If companies behave like this on the brink of war with fascists, it is beyond delusional to harbour any belief that business will ever raise the gauntlet - no matter how much nature bombards us with warnings or scientists slam us with facts.

Yet to deride business would be a folly on our part. The fault lies not with them but the present structure of the market, simply because a company is not paid for being virtuous but for rising sales and higher profit, built around the cut-throat world of competition. And if any company dare stray too far from the path of short-term profit, they become vulnerable to predation.[70]

> *'Competition is industrial war... Ignorant, unrestricted competition carried to its logical conclusion means death to some of the combatants and injury to all.'*[71]

Yet here's Hayek again:

> *'Markets are brilliant means of capturing the collective judgement of individual intelligence because they allow decentralised decision making.'*

These two contrasting views, one from inside the world of business, showing how the process erodes human values, while the other observed from without, if correctly applied expounds capitalism's dazzling and dizzying effect.

So, while it may help to raise people from the poverty trap and bring a cornucopia of material wealth, it fails on a monumental scale on what we collectively judge the greatest ever threat to humanity – *ecological breakdown.*[72]

This blind-spot in our economy has caused many students to lean back and wonder why they are spending four years of their life getting into debt studying economics, when it appears archaic and stunted, leaving a gaping hole in its equation – referring to the environment as a mere *externality.*

Yet fixing this obligates businesses to reverse the very principle that powers them – growth and greater sales. Moreover, the scale required to reverse it would demand near-epic proportions – calling on every boardroom in every business to change the subject of conversation from profit to saving the planet – *'you might as well',* as one friend told me, *'try to persuade a pack of polar bears to change their diet from one of meat to bamboo. It just won't happen!'*

Highly improbable, perhaps, but not impossible. Besides, animals are known to evolve on shifting their diet when the environment demands; and business lives in an environment that runs on artificial numbers, and this is the Age of Information, after all.

6. PEOPLE, POWER & TAX

Societies

Around 5,000 BC, when man threw off the mantle of the hunter-gatherer and began to make settlements, it wasn't long before those settlements grew into towns. Towns then grew into cities which eventually became states. Along every step in this process the human bonds were fraying. No longer were we sharing the intimate experiences of life, be it the journey, partaking in the thrill of the hunt, or gathering around fires. Where once we were closely dependent on one another for our survival, instead we were taking to the field to sow and harvest, building walls and digging wells. Yet we accepted each of these duties as we did the tasks before – to aid one another, prepare, prove to others and ourselves.

But as communities progressed, the process of governing became more complex, for hierarchies were being stretched and governors were becoming isolated from the governed. Leaders were less empathetic and answerable to those around, making for an injudicious power relationship which proved a fertile ground for the ambitious. Armies were quickly raised and these soldiers were not merely to defend against others raiding, but invading too, enabling a leader's power to grow and deal swiftly with those who dared to criticise.

'*Livestock, the boat trade, fishing, even funerals--but probably the most burdensome obligation a household faced was its labour obligation. This was called 'going' or 'burden' in Babylonian languages. A free man, head of his household, owed the government many months of labour service. If he were lucky, his service might entail harvesting the government's barley fields or digging the silt out of canals. If he were unlucky, he had to do military service, leaving the security of home to fight wars abroad, perhaps never to return. Not unnaturally men who could afford it avoided this labour service: they either sent a slave or hired someone on their behalf.*[73]*

As recorded here in ancient Babylonia, this abuse of power resulted from the shortfall of democracy, as people were no longer in a position to contest another's skill or wisdom to govern.

Oppressed by the state, for the state, through tax, people became subjects to the elite, leading to why *tax* has so oft been scorned from the moment of its inception.

Revolts against those in power became common, and more often than not, stamped out. The state, despite its position however, didn't always win.

The declaration in 1215 of the 'Great Charter' – otherwise known as the *Magna Carta* – is a classic case in point. The King of England demanded higher taxes to raise funds for his armies to wage war, *again!* But the Barons, being drained of their resources due to his repeated failings on the battlefield rose up and demanded greater property rights.

Martin Luther, in 1517, on witnessing the mass poverty around him in Germany, publicly questioned the right of the

Catholic Church to charge people for *indulgences*. Soon after, peasants rallied to his call, kicking off the reformation, which later spread throughout all of Northern Europe and beyond, encouraging people to interpret the bible for themselves and not have it interpreted for them, thus allowing them to make up their own minds.

Commonly feted, these two cases are not brief, isolated blips of democracy but part of a series…

During the 1540s, people in France repeatedly and violently rebelled against a salt tax only to be even more violently suppressed.

In 1637, in England, the politician John Hampden stood against the king by refusing to pay tax. Imprisoned, then released only to lose his life in battle. Yet his standing and death resulted in the Monarch being unable to govern without the parliament's consent.

On the other side of the Atlantic, in 1773, the United States was the scene of the Boston Tea Party, a revolt against the British Crown – 'No taxation without representation.'

Uprisings like these show when governors lose favour with the governed their *power* becomes diminished. But as democracy has flourished around the world, you notice from 1950s, interspersed between these protests against the state, public anger has taken a decisive shift where people no longer only demonstrate against the *taking* of what they deem theirs, but what that tax was *used for*.

In 1951 for example, several conscientious objectors (Quakers) from the US, left their homes to found a new settlement in Monteverde, Costa Rica. Their reasoning behind this was they no longer wanted to contribute their taxes when it was spent on the military (Costa Rica had abolished theirs).

In the US again, the Amish community from 1935 to 1965 repeatedly tried to gain exemption from social insurance programs, to which congress eventually made them exempt.

In 1968, 458 writers and editors decided to place full-page adverts in the *New York Post*, *Ramparts* and the *New York Times*, jointly refusing to pay a proposed 10% war tax.

In 1999, the World Trade Organisation's (WTO) annual meeting was held in Seattle, Washington, in what was later called 'The Battle of Seattle'. An estimated 50,000 to 100,000 protesters gathered from all over the world and took to the streets where they marched through the pouring rain. They were there to demonstrate not against war, but for human rights, student rights, religion and the environment.

A year later in Davos, Switzerland, officials, bankers and directors, representing large multinationals arrived from around the globe to take part in the World Economic Forum – the perfect location for protestors to unfurl their annual *SHAME* award, branding corporations for selfishly acting in the pursuit of profit[74]. Amongst those were:

Barclays Bank – shamed for speculating in food prices, causing staple foods to rise at the expense of the poor.

Syngenta – shamed for continuing to sell *Paraquat*, a herbicide banned in the EU for being harmful, despite that thousands of farmers are known to have died from its effects.

Samsung – shamed for using a banned and toxic substance while not protecting and informing its factory workers.

Vale – shamed for constructing a dam in the middle of the Amazon which forced the relocation of 40,000 people without compensating any of them.

Tepco – shamed for neglected safety measures in its nuclear power plants to cut costs despite being Japan's biggest energy company, it has.

Freeport – shamed for operating mines in West Papua that pollute, and turning a blind eye to the torturing of people who raised their voices.

The year after, in Italy, a quarter of a million protestors arrived at the G8 summit in Genoa to make their voices heard.

In 2009-10, students across the University of California took to occupying buildings across the campus to protest at the hikes in tuition fees, budget cuts and staff redundancies caused by the financial crisis.

In Spain, 2011, no less than 15,000 demonstrators marched on the Catalonian Parliament under the banner: 'We are not goods in the hands of politicians and bankers.' Other Protests followed around the country. Some put the figure of those marching as high as 130,000.

In Malaysia that same year, a grassroots movement occupied the streets with the goal of: 'redefining democratic participation beyond representative democracy, and imagining a new political culture beyond race, ideology and political affiliation.'

Shortly after, *Adbusters,* an anti-consumerist magazine based in Vancouver, Canada, presented the idea of occupying Wall Street to protest at how democracy was being unduly influenced by corporations; at how many were suffering through austerity after the public had bailed out the banks; and at the spiralling disparity in wealth. The protest went ahead, spreading to an unprecedented 800 locations (or camps) around the globe. People stood against multinationals and banks, at how they used strategies to benefit the few at the expense of the many. The county of Los Angeles adopted a resolution in support of the movement, and even a board member of the Bank of England, stated they were right to criticise the way banks were *immorally managed*.[75]

In Wales, 2015, the tiny village of Crickhowell went one step further; as a protest against multinationals using tax havens it decided to declare itself a haven.[76] Teaming up with a television show, the village attempted to *offshore* their community in the hope of spurring the government into closing the loopholes that allowed tax avoidance so that its cafes could compete fairly and justly with the likes of the larger chains like Starbucks and Caffe Nero.

From the Magna Carta to the village of Crickhowell, these lessons from history repeatedly show that for all our shared values and beliefs, it is *tax* has an uncanny habit of igniting public anger, many of which have led to the dilution of power into a myriad of different democratic forms.

What's more, these public demonstrations are not just against the government for taking what they consider as theirs, or for investing those funds towards issues they see as unfit, but increasingly the *Multinational* corporations, as they have grown stronger, more powerful, yet shirk due responsibility. Thus, this shift in public resentment mirrors the shift in financial power, exposing both the pull of corporations and the government's failure to correct this.

In 1864, Abraham Lincoln wrote to William Elkins, saying:

'I see in the near future a crisis approaching that unnerves me and cause me to tremble for safety of my country; corporations have been enthroned, an era of corruption in High Places will follow, and the Money Power of the country will endeavour to prolong its reign by working upon the prejudices of the People, until the wealth is aggregated in a few hands, and the Republic destroyed.'

Adam Smith fired a similar caution:

'The proposal of any new law or regulation of commerce which comes from (capitalists) ought always to be listened to with great precaution, and ought never to be adopted, till after having been long and carefully examined, with the most suspicious attention. It comes from an order of men, whose interest is never exactly the same with that of the public, who have generally an interest to deceive and even to oppress the public.'

The nature of business has not changed, yet what puts business under the increased scrutiny of the public's baleful eye is how they have become ever more adept at deceiving, how they lobby, advertise and evade tax through intricate webs, heavily distorting the relationship between the three parties.

It is said that out of the 200 largest economic entities, 157 are now corporations. Walmart, Toyota and Shell all accrue more wealth than even relatively rich countries such as Russia, Belgium or Sweden. *'Global Justice Now'*, a social justice organisation, released these figures in 2018 to pressurise the UK government to push for the UN Treaty, forcing transnational corporations to abide by human rights responsibilities.[77]

But *rights* and *paying tax* don't exactly go hand-in-hand with profits. If a country were to raise taxation or regulations, it threatens a company's competitive advantage and a corporation will simply relocate elsewhere just like the banks do in London, as borders and fences don't exist for a business, but open arms.

Therefore, when searching for a new site, a multinational will factor in the usual tax rates, logistics, wage rates and so forth, yet alongside these is how much that government is willing to turn a blind eye to regulations, effectively creating a bidding war between nations, counties, and even cities or towns,[78] creating a race to the bottom. Thus, competition can be detrimental to the 'public good', contrary to what Adam Smith claimed, as the only party that benefits long-term is business, not the state and certainly not the public.

Neither does it stop there. Peer closer, and after setting up shop you often find corporations altering how they 'book' their income on paper, paying loyalty or licensing fees to other companies located in tax-free havens, which, more often than not, rewinds its way back into the hands of the corporation that paid it! This may sound like wasted energy, but not to business, as it further minimises tax to the state. Apple, for instance, is said to have paid a corporate tax rate of just 0.005% on its European profits in 2014.[79]

And on it goes, the bigger the company the more consistent they are in lobbying, making a highly unlevel playing field for the market, while delivering more power into the hands of multinationals and their board members. According to the IMF, governments lose at least $500 billion to corporations shifting taxes.

Further still, any individual at the corporate helm determined to take a principled stand, would surely be foolish not to cave in and follow, on seeing others get away 'scot-free.'[80] For odds are, in time, they will be swallowed whole by competition, making their investors and staff lose out.

Therefore, the government's duty is to quash these loopholes. In October 2021, 136 countries signed up to do just that. Ensuring corporations pay a minimum of 15% tax. However, it's not all rosy as this is still lower than what smaller businesses pay and corporations will quickly find ways around it.

Yet rather than have the state regressively, chase down corporations that serially misbehave, would it not be more efficient to remedy this situation altogether and redraw where the dividing lines of power really lay, by monetising democracy, through tax?

Democracy?

'Power is ultimately investment decisions.'

Noam Chomsky

As much as money represents power through investment, we must not forget it is a common good. Money allows us to better share and trade what we consider a value, and as such, it acts as a social bond. Yet in acknowledging this, we must too recognise money as an ethical conscience and design a way to realise this.

Today, under the current socio-economic model, the bulk of investment choices can be broadly split between governmental decisions, which focuses on growth and retaining power; Corporate decision-making, designed pretty much exclusively on growth and profits; and consumers, which is much more broad and based upon our immediate needs, pleasures and well-being.

Excluding the public, of the other two, a business chooses where to invest on a day-to-day basis, while governments choose what to tax and where those proceeds go at an altogether slower pace. Business leads and governments follows. Yet in terms of public interest, one is restrained democratically by the will of people for the good of society (be it crudely), while the other is not, and restrained by one thing, *money*.

Indeed, Robert Dahl, Professor of Political Science at Yale University, said this:

'The internal 'governments' of capitalist firms are typically undemocratic; sometimes, indeed, they are virtually

managerial despotisms. Moreover, the ownership of firms and the profits and other gains resulting from ownership are distributed in highly unequal fashion. Unequal ownership and control of major economic enterprises in turn contribute massively to the inequality in political resources.[81]

This reaffirms the consensus from *The Library of Mistakes* along with what is the public's long-held suspicion. Even business itself admits that the power of corporations under the yoke of the financial system they serve, have become decoupled from society, opening a democratic loophole.

Would it not be logical, therefore, to democratise business? After all, our elected governments, the pivot of public finance, consistently pander to business over the public, believing they know best. Besides, they make far more and far larger investment decisions that affect society that government.

Furthermore, Milton Friedman, [82] the klaxon for neoliberalism, believed of an 'inescapable connection between capitalism and democracy.' He saw each represented decentralised empowerment, eroding the risk of dictatorships. Yet today, it is not just dictatorships we should be fearing, but market fundamentalism, since corporations are becoming derailed from their purpose of serving the public, as they serve their makers - shareholders and the board - disproportionately more.

A case in point is ICI (Imperial Chemical Corporation). In the 60s its motto read: 'We want to be the best chemical corporation in the world,' only to change in the 90s: 'We want to maximise shareholder value.'

To strive for perfection in their industry spells *progress*, while to make its CEOs and shareholders exclusively rich, evokes disgust.

Thus, if capitalism and democracy are inescapably entwined around each other like the strands that make up our DNA, one should complement the other and be in balance, not deceive or choke. As such, since democracy is centred around electing representatives that best serve our needs, would it not be better to *select* those businesses that serve us best, rewarding them over others. Besides, our existing model of democracy is far from ideal.

In order for democracy to flourish, there must exist five criteria. Which are:

1. ACTIVE ENGAGEMENT – All citizens have the right to have their voice heard, whether proposing or backing a policy, or that of questioning one.

Today, the public's opinion is generally limited to several or even just two political parties, making you vote (a) not for what you want, but the least bad option. Moreover, this right to vote is only exercised once every four or five years, limiting your engagement even further (b).

Besides, if the party you voted for did go on to win, it is not uncommon for the elected to fail at following up on the policies they pledged (c). Theresa May on winning the Conservative Party leadership, vowed to create a Britain that 'worked for everyone, not just the privileged few', along with getting 'tough on the irresponsible behaviour in big business,' and to deal with the 'unhealthy and growing gap between what corporations pay their workers and what they pay their bosses.'

Nothing happened.

Or say your representative were to push for the policy you voted the party in for, due to the swing of the parliamentary process, these policies are often overturned the following term by their opposites (d) – Trump reversed no less than twenty of

Obama's policies within two-hundred days of office. Only for Biden to reverse much of Trump's. This leads to voter apathy making businesses afraid to invest for fear of getting their finances burnt (e).

2. AN EQUAL RIGHT TO VOTE – All citizens must have an equal vote.

With voting limited to a single day, it can prove too much for many, as they may not have the time nor funds to get to the polling booth (f).

Another erosive issue is that of constituency boundaries. Drawn up to keep the representative beholden to the same number of citizens, it is regularly abused. For in wanting to retain power, incumbents redraw the lines according to the demographics that point to voters who will most likely lean to their party. This *gerrymandering* disenfranchises other voters (g).

3. ENLIGHTENED UNDERSTANDING – Every citizen taking part in an election should be granted the necessary time to understand the policies and their consequences.

In terms of representative democracy, it is rare to have a balanced view from the opposition (h) and take up something more akin to an internecine feud as they attempt to swing voters rather than engage in constructive dialogue. A prime example was Brexit. Posted brazenly on the side of a big red bus, were the words: 'We send the EU £350 million a week. Let's fund our NHS instead, VOTE LEAVE.' Yet on winning, the *leave* campaign immediately backtracked on the funding, showing the public not to be informed, but duped, deliberately. Whereas the *Remainers* claimed our economy would suffer and Brexit would cause a recession. It hasn't, as yet.

Then there are the traditional media outlets such as TV, radio or newspapers, the vast majority of which are owned by billionaires. This enables them to have a strong hand in influencing public opinion (i), which makes them not so much lobby the government, but the government lobby them (j).[83] Ans now with the advance of technology, things have gotten decidedly worse.

The British Electoral Commission, responsible for upholding the law on voting, states that two separate campaigns must not work together unless they declare their expenditure jointly. This is to ensure a level playing field and limit spending, so no one can *buy* an election. However, after Brexit, a close working relationship was uncovered between two data analytical firms employed by two separate campaign groups – *Vote leave & Leave.EU,* which just so happen to be funded by the foreign billionaire, John Mercer – the same US billionaire who backed Donald Trump.

This exposes how the people's sovereignty can be suppressed by the very people a democracy is supposed to restrain – the 1% – thereby affecting our *equal right to vote.*

4. AN OPEN AND ADAPTABLE AGENDA – All citizens have the right to forward any proposals or change existing ones.

Dismissing voting, the more common, traditional way to engage with politics is through party membership, where you would get to discuss the issues at hand and have your say in shaping those policies. However, party membership is shrinking across the globe with people fed-up, and thus the chances of adapting that agenda are shrinking with it. Indeed, the Conservative Party in the UK on electing a new leader in July

2019 for the post of Prime Minister, despite the Tory Party membership only counting for 0.27%[84] of the UK population.[85] The irony here is the RSPB (The Royal Society for the Protection of Birds) has more members than all the political parties put together,[86] revealing people have more in common with feathered birds than they do in having a say shaping their own future!

A different route is to petition, write or visit your representative, laying out the change you want. *If* the representative then opted to take it forward, they have to present it before parliament where it requires a majority to pass.

And then there is the issue of globalisation. Even if available to vote (b) and you agree to a policy your representative wants to put through (c), and he is principled enough not to be coerced by his party (a) or lobbyists (j) as well as having the time to push it through (g & i) instead of investing his time in getting re-elected, he will have little sway (k). Because globalisation has not just changed politics at an international level, but the national level too. For laws have increased under institutions such as the IMF, WTO, EU or UN, making it harder for representatives to bring about specific changes.

5. INCLUSIVITY – Equality must extend to all citizens within the state.

In the United States, the cost of each presidential race comes in at an astounding $6 billion (l); and once in office, members of congress spend between 30–70% of their time attempting to raise money to get re-elected, rather than focus on the job at hand – yes, the one they were elected for (m). What's more, the bulk of that funding comes not from the people or even from the 1%, but the 0.05% who think nothing of donating $10,000 or more (i). Not only does this show that money is a distraction to those who govern, but it controls a large part of the agenda. Another irony here comes in the form of Donald Trump, who in his election mantra cooed, how he – a billionaire – was not beholden to anyone, as he was capable of funding his own campaign and didn't need any favours.

Further still, according to the World Bank, voter turnout across the globe has been continuing to drop for the last 25 years,[87] with people no longer feeling they make any difference.

Some nations attempt to offset this by forcing the public to vote – Australia from the 1920s for example. Yet if people can't bring themselves to vote, what's to say they will ever take the time to reflect on the issues?

In summary:

a) Your opinion is narrowed to the parties on offer, often numbering just two.

b) You only get to voice your opinion once every five or so years.

c) You vote for policies that often fail to come about.

d) Policies are regularly overturned the following term.

e) The system creates despondency, lowering voter turnout.

f) You only get to vote on a single day.

g) The system is prone to gerrymandering.

h) The parties rarely commit to constructive dialogue and play to their audience for political points.

i) The media regularly skews the argument in favour of the 1% - those who own it.

j) Representatives are highly prone to lobbying.

k)   International law allows less room for change.

l)   The sheer lunacy of the cost of elections.

m) Representatives spend so much time trying to retain power that it distracts them from the job in hand.

These challenges expose modern-day democracy to be little short of stunted, and when you add the diminishing power of the state under the present neoliberalist model, the public exercise little in the way of power. Indeed, Freedom House, an independent watchdog that scrutinises elections in 195 countries, said 2020 was 'the 15th consecutive year of decline in global freedom.'[88]

Therefore, given the sheer struggle in trying to get your voice heard, would it not make sense to bypass the parliamentary procedure altogether and avoid every one of these challenges and go straight to where power is exercised over us the most, *the boardroom.*

'The institution that most changes our lives we least understand, or, more correctly, seek most elaborately to understand… week by week, month by month, year by year, it exercises a greater influence on our livelihood and the way we live than unions, universities, politicians and governments.'

John Kenneth Galbraith, 1977,
referring to Corporations.

Let's Get Down to Business

Spare a look at the issues in the UK 2019 election.[89]

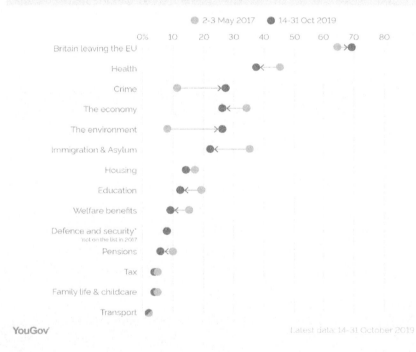

Environment and crime are seen as much bigger issues now than they were at the same point in the 2017 election campaign
Which of the following do you think are the most important issues facing the country at this time? Please tick up to three. %

● 2-3 May 2017   ● 14-31 Oct 2019

Britain leaving the EU	
Health	
Crime	
The economy	
The environment	
Immigration & Asylum	
Housing	
Education	
Welfare benefits	
Defence and security* *not on the list in 2017	
Pensions	
Tax	
Family life & childcare	
Transport	

YouGov   Latest data: 14-31 October 2019

Now compare them to the US voters in 2016.[90]

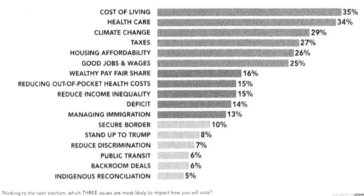

TOP 3 ISSUES IMPACTING YOUR VOTE

COST OF LIVING	35%
HEALTH CARE	34%
CLIMATE CHANGE	29%
TAXES	27%
HOUSING AFFORDABILITY	26%
GOOD JOBS & WAGES	25%
WEALTHY PAY FAIR SHARE	16%
REDUCING OUT-OF-POCKET HEALTH COSTS	15%
REDUCE INCOME INEQUALITY	15%
DEFICIT	14%
MANAGING IMMIGRATION	13%
SECURE BORDER	10%
STAND UP TO TRUMP	8%
REDUCE DISCRIMINATION	7%
PUBLIC TRANSIT	6%
BACKROOM DEALS	6%
INDIGENOUS RECONCILIATION	5%

Thinking to the next election, which THREE issues are most likely to impact how you will vote?

And here are the issues in Australia, 2018.[91]

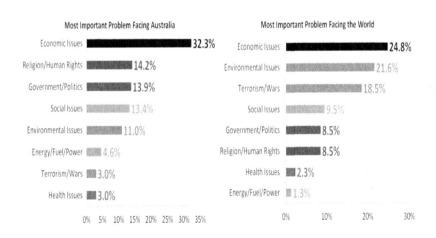

Most Important Problem Facing Australia

Economic Issues	32.3%
Religion/Human Rights	14.2%
Government/Politics	13.9%
Social Issues	13.4%
Environmental Issues	11.0%
Energy/Fuel/Power	4.6%
Terrorism/Wars	3.0%
Health Issues	3.0%

0% 5% 10% 15% 20% 25% 30% 35%

Most Important Problem Facing the World

Economic Issues	24.8%
Environmental Issues	21.6%
Terrorism/Wars	18.5%
Social Issues	9.5%
Government/Politics	8.5%
Religion/Human Rights	8.5%
Health Issues	2.3%
Energy/Fuel/Power	1.3%

0% 10% 20% 30%

Given that Brexit and Trump were respectively unique to the UK and US, of all the other concerns, they are broadly similar. Yet, when you pause to consider if business were to come under any form of democratic governance, it would come laden with its own fresh challenges.

To start, a business has little influence over policies like foreign policy or healthcare, and the same could be said of immigration or education. As to terrorism, gun control, abortion or drugs, a business would dismally fail. Yet name one single business that does not contribute to the economy or is able to do its bit and help stop the markets push us further down the road to ecological breakdown?

What's more, compared to the majority of public concerns these are not lay or divisive issues[92] as they affect each and every one of us.

1) Climate change is not just a risk to the economy and our lifestyle but poses an existential threat.

2) People are worried or extremely worried the world over.[93]

3) Above all, the first duty of any government is to protect its people.

As to the economy, it is commonly the number one issue on the agenda or in the top three issues, for voters the world over. Not that people want a stronger economy per se, but the benefits they perceive it will bring them – jobs and promotion, along with all the trappings. However, a growing economy doesn't necessarily deliver these. But one thing does, *investment*.

According to Professor Robert Solow, the Nobel laureate, 80% of economic growth persistently comes down to research and development, which demands *long-term investment*.[94] However, up until the 1980s, the US corporate sector averaged 4% of GDP, while dividends were 2%. Today that figure is reversed. Furthermore, 40% of the US stock market is now owned by the 1%, and a very high proportion of those funds are reinvested back into it, rather than fed back through what is the real economy. Thus, a stronger economy does not automatically carry in its wake greater social mobility, unless of course you are in that wealthiest 1%.

The price of a company on Wall Street indicates its relative size and what investors believe its future earnings will be. An executive's pay and bonus scheme are often linked to this to encourage him/her to drive the company forward. However, this causes the board to concentrate on short-term and high-risk strategies, discouraging long-term investment. A recent example of this is Persimmon,[95] a company that builds domestic houses in the UK. Its share price doubled over several years which resulted in its CEO walking away with a bonus of £100 million. Yet the price soared not on account of the quality of its houses,[96] nor for his skill and vision in steering the company, but because its sales - 48% of their houses were purchased through the 'help-to-buy' scheme, a policy set-up by the government to assist those with less income afford a home of their own, which only went to raise the prices of houses further. This not only caused a nationwide rise in house sales, but the share price of Persimmon. Now juxtapose the CEO'S earnings to the profit the company reportedly made on each house: £66,265.[97]

Wrong, irrational and outdated, sky-high pay packets such as these have become common the world over. What's more, it comes at a time when houses should be built to both prepare and reduce the effects of the planetary crisis. If every Persimmon house were fitted with triple glazing, fully insulated, fixed with solar panels, ground source heat-pumps, grey water recycling systems and so forth, not only would each house be cutting their carbon footprint - and bills - but Persimmon would still have made a very handsome profit on every house, enabling their CEO to walk off with a healthy bonus all the same, not a ridiculously, stupid sum for no sensible reason.[98]

Instead, the UK housing stock is amongst the poorest insulated in Europe.[99] Indeed, as I write, members of 'Insulate Britain,' a protest group are blocking roads around the country, not demanding more pay or to stop a war, but to make the government fully insulate houses to lower our carbon footprint and save household bills.[100]

Yet, so long as regulations remain slack and the financial system remains unrestrained, boardrooms will continue to favour board members and shareholders - those who control the reins of power - not steering us towards a brighter future.

So, is order to change this and stop business exploiting their position and get them to invest in what benefits us?

The Five Paths

Every business sell products or services to create revenue, whether they are material or intangible goods. Then to operate a business requires labour and energy, materials to create and a stable site to work from. Once it has these, it seeks the path that offers the quickest route to the highest return, which can generally be narrowed down to five:[101]

1. Core design – research & innovation.

2. Operating costs – efficiency.

3. Sales – advertising & distribution.

4. Price – its adjustment based on market research.

5. Minimising tax.

What's clear here is certain paths have greater potential than others to benefit society by bringing about a cleaner, more sustainable environment. Therefore, would it not be cannier to nudge them off certain paths and onto those that help prevent and prepare for climate change, thus softening the challenges that lay ahead, rather than have the government continue to dish out what are in effect regressive regu7lations and have the taxpayer foot the bill?

The eco-label already performs this task of course, by exposing part of the efficiency/core design of the goods at the time of purchase. However, its weakness is in how it does not wield sufficient influence over all five paths, allowing business to crisscross from one path to another in its continued pursuit of short-term profit.

Starting from the bottom (5), when it comes to evading or avoiding tax[102] it angers many people. Eighty-nine percent of adults in the UK say tax avoidance is morally wrong.[103] Of the small minority that disagree, they believe failing to pay tax has a higher chance of creating jobs as the company will grow, making funds feed back into the economy. However, whether the funds get fed back in or not, it has a detrimental effect morally/economically, for when a business avoids tax, it not only encourages others to follow suit, but the extra burden is placed on the yoke of others and issues like infrastructure starts to fall down, requiring yet higher tax.

As to (4), when it comes to increasing or decreasing prices, it is widely believed that businesses cut prices of competition, bringing down the price for consumers. But price adjustments are not wholly made on these grounds but go the other way — to squeeze more from consumers to maximise profit, as companies raise prices to look classy.[104] Furthermore, when a business outmanoeuvres other competitors in price, it can show little or no benefit to society, as it so often fails to *improve* the product.

Advertising (3) was created to help consumers identify a product, but soon crossed a moral line as businesses realised that by weaving a wonderful story it made the packaging stand out and sales increased, which was far cheaper than researching and improving the actual product's design.

What's more, like tax avoidance, it angers people. Today, it's believed upwards of $760 billion is spent each and every year on advertising,[105] making it an assault against reason given our predicament and its central purpose.

This leaves innovation and efficiency (1&2), the core benefits of what capitalism is *supposed* to deliver better than any other economic/political system. The fruits of which benefit humanity the most. It is through these two paths that an economy can be stimulated, leading to a greener, more sustainable future, serving our greatest needs.[106]

A prime example of bad investment is what happened in Detroit in the sixties.

Once *the* major automobile manufacturing hub in the world - if only it were to last. The boardrooms learnt that higher profits could be had using tactical advertising (3) rather than directing their energies into delivering cleaner, more efficient and reliable engines (1&2). They did this by introducing new bodywork designs and colours, which in its essence, is nothing more than placing new shells on top of existing engines and marketing them as new! This duping of the public made them believe they were buying the latest technology, and in 1973, when the oil crisis struck and the price of fuel shot skywards, the public realised they had been conned. Dropping their American Gas Guzzlers with a heavy loss or scrapping them completely, they switched to the cleaner and greener Japanese and German models and Detroit sank like a stone. Today, however, it is not an oil crisis we are sleepwalking into, but climate change, which is where the current structure of neoliberalism falls down.

Cutting pollution by making transport ever more efficient, reliable and safe, is substantially more beneficial than merely altering the character of the bodywork – both to a client's pocket and their health, along with the long-term benefit to society. Every year, 4.2 million premature deaths are attributed to air pollution.[107]

However, the CEOs at Detroit chose to sacrifice what are basic human values to generate greater profits by giving the public what they wanted without laying out all the facts i.e., deliberately deceiving them. Milton Friedman, for one, insisted there is nothing wrong with this arrangement:

> *'Since markets express the will of the people, virtually any criticism of business could be described as an act of despicable contempt for the common man.'*

This is at best short-sighted as it counters what he said about the market and democracy having a close connection. In a healthy democracy, it is a prerequisite to be properly *informed* before placing a vote.

Secondly, a large void exists between what the public truly wants and what the market churns out. Yet the duty of business is to serve the public, not vice-versa. Therefore, it is only right for them to have their say at the design stage (*active engagement*), not restricted to what business cooks up - which is rather like being served a leftover meal where all the best ingredients were consumed prior to serving.

In essence, the CEOs of Detroit - and still today - focused upon pleasing what the customer sees at face value (the instinctual side), not the *individual* and *society* as a whole (the rational side). Without an informed public having their say, it enables board members to act more like burglars than captains of industry, which helps to explain how our trust in corporations, brands and governments has been eroding and the boardroom's *values* are side-lined by their pursuit of growth.

'The decadent international but individualistic capitalism, in the hands of which we found ourselves after the war, is not a success. It is not intelligent, it is not beautiful, it is not just, it is not virtuous… It gives us what we want, serving us all our wanton desires, but not what we need. Tapping into our instinctual nature.'

Maynard Keynes

On the 8th October 2018 the IPCC[108] declared we have just *'12 years left'* to change direction or face catastrophic consequences.[109] Economic growth is no longer aligned with reality, making that credendum we all sign up to: 'to study hard, work hard and abide by the rules for a brighter future,' no longer valid, ushering in an era of confusion, discord and blame.

Just open any newspaper and you don't have to flip through many pages before one headline shouts things like: 'The Australian central bank shifted to a more cautious outlook amid concerns that steep falls in house prices and the slowdown in China could choke domestic growth,' while another pops up of scientists – our modern-day sages – ringing the alarm: 'Even if we stop burning fossils fuels tomorrow our planet will go on heating up for possibly another 150 years and the oceans, a thousand or more.'

Once headlines such as these were marginalised, but now mainstream. This naturally causes people to turn to politicians, only for them to repeatedly duck and pass the buck to business who quickly snap: 'We're just giving consumers what they want' and 'It's not illegal. We don't set these rules.'[110]

So people turn back again to politicians who retort: 'Listen, we need less intervention. A free market creates jobs and growth remember, and growth's what's needed! Without growth we would never have developed so far and fast.' And if the public wade into the fight and point at business, 'We lobby for our interests, sure,' cries business. 'But those interests are represented by staff like you! Along with our shareholders who trust us to fight for their hard-earned pensions!'

And fight they certainly do. The European Commission claim 15,000 lobbyists operate on behalf of big business in Brussels alone.[111]

Yet isn't it the task of every government to create channels to bring about a better, more just society, while addressing our greatest needs? In any democratised nation, much of that time is vested in trying to cling to power rather than dealing with the issues at hand. Which makes politicians every bit a product of this short-term environment as everybody else. Or *if* any politician were to actually become brave enough to plough through the lobbyists and bring about reform, they are always shouted down: 'Tamper with the market and you'll give our competitors abroad an unfair advantage,' and 'The local economy is dangerously poised right now. You know what that'll lead to – redundancies, in your constituency!'

And the public, what of them? After all the buck stops with them, right? They could always boycott certain brands or demonstrate against an elected body. However, rather than grasp the scales of justice and take up the sword, if it's 10% cheaper and available now, they will gladly settle for *immediate value*. So long as they're not informed, too much.

> '*The incurable narrowness of the soul, that makes people prefer the immediate to the remote.*'
>
> David Hume

The more you read the news and reflect, the more you come to realise how we are all ignoring our collective needs, kowtowing to our most fickle desires, as it is this which business taps into.

But here's the thing, ask any party what their primary purpose or role is in life? The public will most likely sprout something akin to: 'To give back to society and pass my values and beliefs on to my children,' while politicians declare: 'To distribute justice' or 'Raise living standards for all.' While business so often in their mantra coos: 'To act responsibly and provide quality at an affordable price.'

So, it appears that, for all our values and beliefs and the good that we intend, all three parties have become oppressed by the overpowering drive of our economy to grow and grab, pushing aside what defines us best; our beliefs and human values.

But it doesn't have to be this way.

Imagine for a moment, if every business, instead of honing in on our appetites, impulses and base desires, focused upon bringing out what represents the best in us? Wouldn't this make for a more just society, putting *civil* back into *civil*isation. By that same token, what if every business focused on preventing the planetary crisis as much as they do on profit, wouldn't this be the kind of society you want to be a part of, where we work to create a brighter, fairer future, instead of an economy that is placing our very future in serious doubt?

As distant and far-flung as this sounds, it isn't, because the solution lies in the roots of the problem itself, Neoliberalism, and the *price!*

PART 3
THE SOLUTION

NEO-ECO-LIBERALISM

7. MERGING FINANCIAL WITH HUMAN VALUES

Aligning the Five Paths

'Profit is always highest in countries which are going fastest to ruin.'

Adam Smith, Wealth of Nations.

'Where effective competition can be created, it is a better way of guiding individual efforts than any other. It does not deny, but even emphasises that, in order that competition should work beneficially, a carefully thought-out legal frame-work is required, and that neither the existing nor the past legal rules are free from grave defects....'

Frederick Von Hayek

What both economists are drawing our attention to is giving business free rein to pursue its own desires inevitably leads it to opt for the path of least resistance - the autopilot of nature. In other words, it aims to deliver the greatest profits exclusively for the boardroom and investors within the shortest time, while shirking society's wider concerns which it abandons to government and the consumer. Today, however, it is no longer simply a question of pursuing exclusive, linear growth and relying on the invisible hand, but our survival. According to the chair of the Global Assessment Report on Biodiversity & Ecosystem Services, 'we are now eroding the very foundations of our economies, livelihoods, food security, health and quality of life.'

With governments consistently locked in debate over how best to deal with climate change, we already are past the ideal time to change the course of our economies, but we are not yet past the point of no return and can still redirect the flow of what we deem *value*.

By far the most well-tested and efficient method to achieve this is to turn up the competition, but *on our terms;* to reward those companies who serve society best, not expropriate from it. In other words, reversing the type of policies Detroit used to exploit our ignorance, so they invest in the practices and technology that is best geared towards reducing CO_2 and pollution, through their base instinct, *the bottom line.*

> *'There is one and only one social responsibility of business – to use its resources and engage in activities designed to increase its profits.'*

> Milton Friedman.

But dealing with the long-term effects of ecological breakdown is opposed to value as they see it – a whale won't pay business, nor have bees evolved fingers to hit the buy button. So what price do you put on fossil fuels... an alpine meadow... a tree... a drop in the ocean perhaps? This is and always has been something of a Sisyphean task. Besides, it would cause the value of a product to artificially be inflated through the price, and if one nation pursues this, it puts its enterprises at a disadvantage over those in other nation-states.

Neo-ECO-liberalism – or *NEL* – skips this altogether, as it seeks not to value the Earth in its entirety but what a business extracts *compared to its competitors*, thus rewarding or penalising them through the supply chain and displaying it openly for consumers and the public.

Throughout history it's tax that has paved the way for many of the freedoms we enjoy today. In fact, you could say the history of the state is just as much the history of tax – you cannot have one without the other. Tax also provides the strongest, most practical link to tether the state, business and people together, as it redistributes wealth towards *our* needs and goals, or the opposite, if misused. Further still it is tax that has the ability to cut deep into the balance sheet, acting as an incentive and disincentive alike – both to consumers and corporations. Furthermore, it has the power to not just influence *all* five paths, but represents a path itself.

And out of all taxes yet devised, it is sales tax in particular – or its younger cousin, V.A.T. (Value Added Tax) – that represents the strongest link between all parties while being the most active, immediate and publicly visible, crucially making it easier for the public to associate behaviour with brands.

What NEL does is tweak the VAT, making it variable, and bases the rate upon how green the product is; how clean its production process when compared to its peers, and fastens that data to the eco-label.

Currently, with sales tax set at a universal rate for virtually all goods, its task is merely to raise funds for the treasury, which it then redistributes for developmental projects in the wider society. But if VAT were made variable and opened to competition, based upon efficiency and waste (the medium any business can partake and compete in except economic growth), once set, it does more than raise funds, as it encourages businesses to factor in the collective *demands* and *values* of society too, thus sharpening capitalism's wider social vision through assimilating many of the societal/environmental externalities into the creative capitalist process at the design stage i.e., leveraging technologies designed to enhance sustainability as opposed to aim exclusively for short-term profit. Furthermore, this avoids the government paying for the clean-up, which is both inefficient, regressive and socialist in outlook.

What's more, in creating this tighter bond between all three parties it promotes trust, justice and accountability, In other words, instead of putting profit before principles, or principles before profit, it helps to end this eternal wrangle - aligning the boardroom's will closer to society's ills - not inflaming this point of friction.

And from a democratic perspective:

1. ACTIVE ENGAGEMENT – In regards to the economy and the environment, they are non-divisive, as we all want a more robust economy and need a healthy and stable environment. But the issue has always been at what cost? What NEL does is get businesses that tread heavier to contribute more to this compared to those who tread lighter. This effectively throws it to the market to solve while shifting the burden away from the taxpayer, redirecting our brightest minds to solving the greatest problem we face, as opposed to shifting money from A to B.

2. THE EQUAL RIGHT TO VOTE – On every purchase made, unwittingly or not, a consumer will effectively be helping to change the two key issues of concern, thus partaking in the democratic process on a daily basis, not voting once every five years based on what can be vague policies.

3. ENLIGHTENED UNDERSTANDING – The eco-label improves transparency, revealing which corporations are helping to tackle issues we care about - or not - informing the public better where their money is directed.

4. AN OPEN AND ADAPTABLE AGENDA – Putting a halt to climate change is in all our interests, making this null and void.

5. INCLUSIVITY – Power is extended to any citizen who can shop, regardless of education, colour, race, age or gender.

And now take a look at it from the viewpoint of business through the five paths.

1. Core design – research/innovation.

2. Operating costs – efficiency.

3. Sales – advertising & distribution.

4. Price – its adjustment based on market research.

5. Minimising tax.

Out of the various scenarios you can play out under this policy, chief among them is how path (5) contains the necessary gravitas to affect all other paths, as it alters the common strategy a business employs by pushing for higher environmental standards.

A variable VAT rate offers an entirely new way to gain a competitive advantage over rivals while earning brands kudos. However, the price of such a move comes only through (2) greater efficiency and (1) innovation – that is, creating cleaner and greener production processes, products and packaging etc. Failing to pursue this path will essentially cause a brand to lose its lustre (through the label), thus affecting sales (3) while becoming more expensive in the process (4) as it will be taxed higher (5).

In other words, if a business were to disproportionately concentrate on paths 3 & 4, the competition from other companies in focusing on path 5 and investing in innovating greener products, processing or packaging, will have a greater financial return as it brings down the direct price of their goods, putting at a disadvantage any company that hones in on marketing and price adjustments.

Varying Value Added Tax

Value Added Tax (VAT), in its essence, is a form of consumer tax like that of sales tax in the US, just more protracted.

Take an everyday piece of furniture such as a coffee table. It would typically follow a path of production by starting at a supplier before heading to the factory floor, after which a retailer would purchase it who would put it on his/her display space where a consumer would buy it.

Sales tax works on the basis that it is only the end-user (the consumer) who gets charged the tax, and it is the sole task of the retailer to apply it, which they then pay to the government treasury.

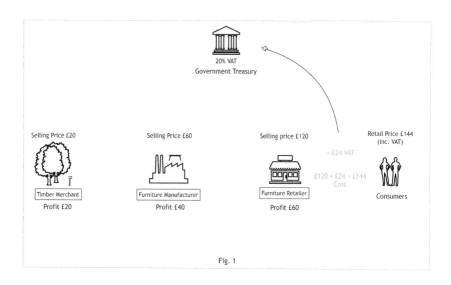

Fig. 1

In figure 2 below, you will see that VAT on the other hand is charged at each stage of the supply-chain. In this case the manufacturer has a sum of £12 (20% on the sale price of £60) to pay which it gets from the retailer, who it then forwards it to the treasury. This is repeated along every stage with the exception of the end-user.

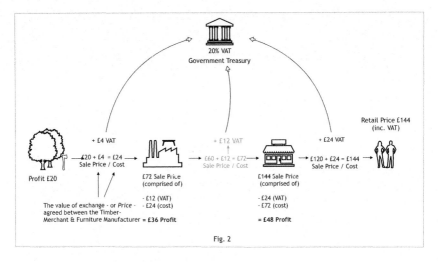

Fig. 2

However, at every link in the supply-chain (except the end-user) the business responsible for charging and forwarding the tax to the treasury can reclaim that VAT upon retaining proof of the receipt, showing the date, the price paid and the VAT.

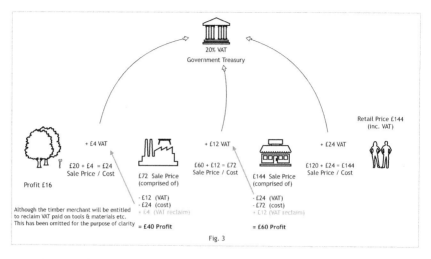

20% VAT
Government Treasury

Retail Price £144
(inc. VAT)

+ £4 VAT
£20 + £4 = £24
Sale Price / Cost
Profit £16

+ £12 VAT
£60 + £12 = £72
Sale Price / Cost
£72 Sale Price
(comprised of)

+ £24 VAT
£120 + £24 = £144
Sale Price / Cost
£144 Sale Price
(comprised of)

Although the timber merchant will be entitled
to reclaim VAT paid on tools & materials etc.
This has been omitted for the purpose of clarity

- £12 (VAT)
- £24 (cost)
+ £4 (VAT reclaim)
= £40 Profit

- £24 (VAT)
- £72 (cost)
+ £12 (VAT reclaim)
= £60 Profit

Fig. 3

Despite being a protracted sum requiring extra bookwork, it is the preferred choice in over one hundred and sixty nations worldwide, compared to a few that still retain sales tax. This is down to VAT having several benefits.

Firstly, with VAT raised and paid at every stage in the development of a product, if at any stage a business were to evade paying tax, the treasury will get to collect tax at the other stages, thereby avoiding a full hit.

Secondly, tax evasion is made much harder as it is in the interest of both the vendor and purchaser to retain their receipts to claim back that tax. As such, if one party were to avoid paying while the other does, it exposes the shortfall of the other, thus making evasion riskier for would-be fraudsters.

Thirdly, compared to sales tax, it leaves a trail that is much easier for auditors and inspectors to trace.

Now let's look at how a variable VAT system can operate under this system.

Let's say the manufacturer has an exemplary record of sustainability and really does care about its public image in society.

Its roof is not only green but can sustain thick foliage, promoting biodiversity in the area while guarding against floods. It installed high-grade solar panels too, helping to draw less energy from the national grid. A grey-water recycling system for the production process was erected, recycling 90% of its waste. The table it produces is made from locally sourced material of a durable design, using environmentally friendly dyes. It is also modular and can double up as a desk, serving two purposes. The company uses minimal packaging and its entire delivery fleet is powered using electric vehicles. Through these combined benefits, it is awarded a high eco-label, qualifying it for a reduced rate of 17% (A) as opposed to the standard rate of 20%.

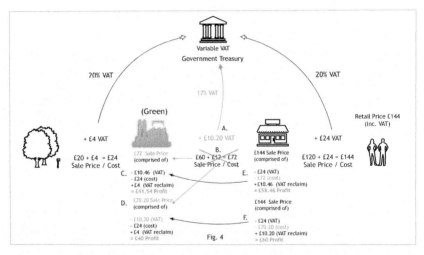

Fig. 4

Because of this, instead of paying £12 in VAT to the treasury, it reduces that bill to £10.20 on every table it sells, thus giving it the choice of increasing its profit margin by £1.54 to retain the current sale price (C) or passing that reduction on to the retailer by reducing the price and gaining a double advantage over competitors by having cheaper and greener goods (D).

Restructuring VAT this way, although attractive at first sight, is flawed, for despite the retailer instantly recognising the manufacturer's goods as greener and cheaper, when examining the invoice, the retailer will notice the benefit is virtually taken (E & C) as they are not able to reclaim the same amount of VAT as before (£10.54 as opposed to £12.00). Alternatively, if the manufacturer passes the benefit on, it merely retains the same margin of profit anyway (F & D), which is £60.

Now let's examine it from a different viewpoint and say two of the links in the chain have been awarded the best eco-label – the manufacturer and the retailer.

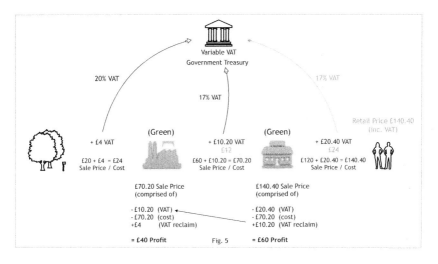

Fig. 5

In this scenario you will notice a price reduction all the way through the chain to the consumers at the end, thereby rewarding both the retailer and manufacturer an advantage over their competitors, enabling them to retain their margin of profit.

However, as much as every business wants to go green to reduce costs and deliver for the greater good, having two links in the chain makes little difference, as seen in Fig 6. As the price remains the same to the customer if the retailer is green in isolation.

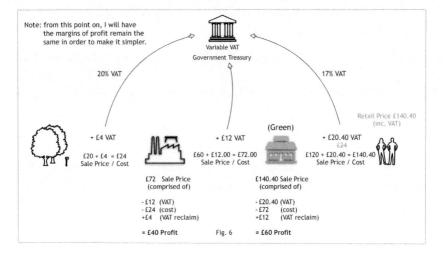

Note: from this point on, I will have the margins of profit remain the same in order to make it simpler.

Variable VAT
Government Treasury

20% VAT   17% VAT

(Green)

Retail Price £140.40
(inc. VAT)

+ £4 VAT   + £12 VAT   + £20.40 VAT
                                              £24
£20 + £4 = £24   £60 + £12.00 = £72.00   £120 + £20.40 = £140.40
Sale Price / Cost   Sale Price / Cost   Sale Price / Cost

£72   Sale Price   £140.40 Sale Price
(comprised of)   (comprised of)

- £12 (VAT)   - £20.40 (VAT)
- £24 (cost)   - £72   (cost)
+£4   (VAT reclaim)   +£12   (VAT reclaim)

= £40 Profit   Fig. 6   = £60 Profit

Now let's look at it from the perspective of having one toxic link and one green.

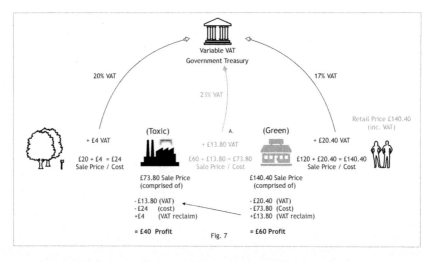

Variable VAT
Government Treasury

20% VAT   17% VAT

23% VAT

(Toxic)   A.   (Green)

Retail Price £140.40
(inc. VAT)

+ £4 VAT   + £13.80 VAT   + £20.40 VAT

£20 + £4 = £24   £60 + £13.80 = £73.80   £120 + £20.40 = £140.40
Sale Price / Cost   Sale Price / Cost   Sale Price / Cost

£73.80 Sale Price   £140.40 Sale Price
(comprised of)   (comprised of)

- £13.80 (VAT)   - £20.40 (VAT)
- £24   (cost)   - £73.80 (Cost)
+£4   (VAT reclaim)   +£13.80 (VAT reclaim)

= £40 Profit   Fig. 7   = £60 Profit

Let us suggest it doesn't just reward companies for sustainability but penalises those that fail to invest in going green. Say the manufacturer has a repeated record of being fined through dumping excess, contaminated water into the river; is a heavy emitter of emissions and does not use recyclates which, altogether, points it to being something of a cash cow rather than a catalyst of change. For these reasons the business has been downgraded and hit with a toxic label, giving it a 23% tax rate.

Keeping the margins of profitability the same, you will notice it neither acts as a disincentive nor incentive for other companies to source from, over greener companies. Despite the toxic goods being more expensive to purchase, the retailer can still reclaim the higher rate of tax directly back from the government anyway, while still managing to sell on the goods to the consumers at a cheaper price through the eco-label. As such, the only incentive is to be had through marketing, making the variable rate's effectiveness null and void.

So, from observing Figs 1-7, it is safe to assume that this model makes a variable VAT rate act as an incentive in isolation, but fails to pass on any monetary benefit when reclaiming the VAT as part of a supply chain. Therefore, if sales tax (as used in the US) were to become variable – as opposed to VAT – being decoupled from the supply chain, it would appear to be more effective in sending a message to business while at the same time, simpler to operate.

However, its chief drawback is how it allows for an increased chance of businesses abusing the system due to the increased competition; and with sales tax being harder to monitor than VAT, it would not make an ideal model.

Therefore, the best way to resolve this is to make the percentage of tax reclaimable for business, the opposite of what it qualifies for in a reduction above and below the average rate of VAT.

For example, if a business were to be rated green (17% in this case) and we have it reclaim back 23% from the government; and if a business is below par and rated toxic (23%) it claims back only 17%.

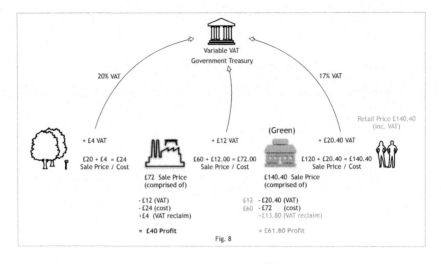

Fig. 8

If we were to expand this model (Fig 9) to include three differently rated retailers which order goods from three contrasting manufacturers, you will observe it pays for the business to source greener goods as well as invest more sustainably. What's more, the price for greener goods at the end of the chain will have a higher probability of being cheaper for consumers (A) and so the climate benefits from a market that prioritises environmental protection and improvement.

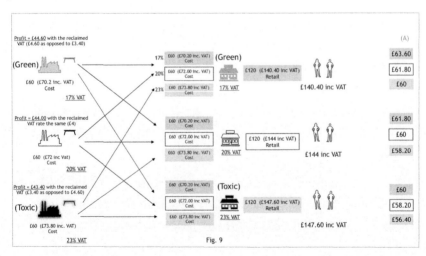

Fig. 9

To make the benefits more transparent, take a look at Fig. 10. In freezing the retail price (A) you can see the profit rise (C to B) making what are strong and clear incentives for industry to move in the direction the public want and how they can profit from it.

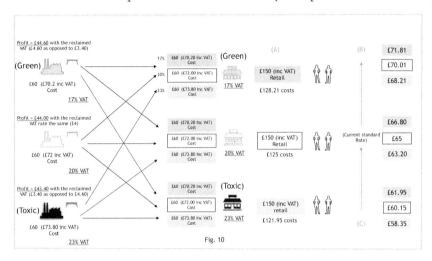

Fig. 10

With tax structured in this manner, sustainability levels across each and every industrial sector will inevitably rise as businesses will continually seek to profit from preventing the crisis.

The Eco Label

Imagine having scoured the market to locate the *type* of product you want in terms of use, design, colour and size. Somewhere amongst that, your eyes will inevitably flick to the *price*. If upon accepting this, and with less emphasis, your eyes switch to the brand's *reliability*, *availability* and eventually, somewhere near the bottom, you just may look into how *green and local* that company is. It is this placing of sustainability at the back of the queue as an afterthought, which has helped land us in the predicament we are in.

Now take a look from the same perspective, but under NEL. Once you have found the *type* of goods you want, the eco-label will have an immediate effect upon you as a purchaser, for:

- A colour signal and location of the arrow denotes you are choosing the right path while offering a higher chance of being cheaper.

- In addition to paying less tax when purchasing, your business will claim a higher sum of money back.

- Added to this, it will contribute to your own product's appeal in being greener, making it more marketable to other businesses further along the chain as well as being cheaper for the end-purchaser.

- Lastly, as well as having an intrinsic value (creating a higher profit for your company), it will also contain an extrinsic value for it brings a positive feedback for society and the environment, both now and in the future.

It is clear from this that the eco-label will nudge the purchaser in a similar way to the subliminal advertising of today.

However, whereas the latter is exclusively based upon a company's ability to focus on growth and profit, the former acts on what we as a society value beyond our, *base instinct*.

Yet it must be said although greener goods will be reduced in price, there is nothing to stop companies thereafter raising prices. A surge in demand will follow as other manufacturers give chase through reducing prices or innovating and pushing for greater efficiency. However, for those that opt not to reduce their VAT, it will inevitably be much harder to play catch-up over time, as corporations will be scrambling to reduce their VAT. Thus, the least inefficient/innovative businesses, will inevitably fall behind, creating, in turn, an opening for the greener businesses to take over.[112]

This is Darwinian economics – predatory, commercial greed – but contingent upon making our future safer.

Despite these two policies presenting such a compelling case, fresh challenges arise.

How to Calculate the Varied Rates?

How to Make Competition Fair?

Quantifying Sustainability & How to Kickstart it?

Assessing & Monitoring Business Sustainability

Globalisation

Public Acceptance

8. HOW TO CALCULATE THE VARYING RATES

Money

When asked to define money, the answer seems immediately obvious – coins and notes. Yet if you were to peer back through history, its apparent that money has always been something of a shapeshifter.

Salt, for example, was used from Africa to China. Cowrie shells from America to Africa and Asia to Britain. Feathers were utilised in parts of the pacific, twisted spearheads in Africa and cigarettes in post-war Germany. And on the list goes… dolphin teeth, cattle,[113] slaves, mackerel,[114] cider, tobacco – all have been used at one time or another. So, being impossible to define by form, it would be more correct to define *money* by its functions.

Firstly, it's primary use is as a *medium of exchange,*[115] *a store* and *measurer of value.* It can also be used to *advance credit.*

It was for these reasons why salt was a good unit of exchange. It had a *universal appeal* and was in high demand and had an intrinsic value. It also never went off and could be easily split and weighed.

Cowrie shells were small, durable and easy to carry; pleasing to the eye and used in jewellery and decoration.

At around 550 BC in Lydia (modern-day Turkey), a new form of money appeared and quickly took hold – *coins*.

These could be stored easier and unlike salt they couldn't mix sand or grit into them. What is more, unlike cowrie shells, because the metal was impressionable, different denominations could be stamped upon its face, backed with an image of the king declaring his authority or brand. This guaranteed the weight and the purity and moved the responsibility away from the tradesmen to the ruler, making Lydia an attractive place to do business and gave the world its first gold standard.

Despite these benefits, they were, and still are, vulnerable to forgery. Clipping, was the most common form, where counterfeiters would 'clip off' the edge of the coins to re-melt them with a cheaper metal and repress new ones. Despite the time they have been in existence, it was not until 1696 when clipping receded with the help of none other than Sir Isaac Newton.

After being appointed Warden of the Mint, Newton recognised that clipping came at a considerable cost to the treasury, which he put a stop to in two ways.

Firstly, in making the coin perfectly round, it made the clipping more pronounced and noticeable. This was achieved by using machines to do the pressing, thereby eliminating human error.

Secondly, he took to serrating its edge, making it harder to tamper with.

Combined, these made the task more difficult and time-consuming for fraudsters. Despite this, forging still continues. In 2014, three-percent of the coins were found to be counterfeit.

Coins had other problems too. Most notably, they are a hindrance when undertaking a transaction of high expense, as they are heavy to hold and carry when in large numbers.

In England around 1100 AD, this was countered using *tally sticks*. Unlike most forms of money, they had no intrinsic value as they were made of hazel or willow and were in a very plentiful supply. However, its unique quality was… well, it's 'uniqueness.' Each branch was unique in colour and texture, along with the pattern of the grain. But best of all, was when snapped in two only those two pieces would fit together again. This made them exceptionally good at keeping records of a contract, given there were just too many variables – the grain, burrs, colour, thickness, length – which made them impossible to forge.

The transactions went something like this: On both parties agreeing to the terms of exchange they would notch the wood to show the pounds, shillings and pence, and then split them. The larger half – *the stock* – was passed to the party that advanced the money, while the shorter part – *the foil* – represented the debtor.

But it was its very uniqueness that proved its downfall, for despite being excellent in the use of bilateral trading, they were not universally transferable and as such completely died out by the 1840s. As a measurer of value and *record* however, they were a very sophisticated form of account-keeping and performed better than coins in *advancing credit*.

The other medium to counter the drawbacks of coins is still used today, paper, and were first used where paper was invented.

Around 650 AD, Chinese merchants would deposit their coins with bankers, and the bankers would print promissory notes which could later be redeemed. However, it wasn't until the 11th century when the government began printing paper money on a large scale thanks to the new technology of the time – woodblock printing.

Ever since coins and notes have been in widespread use and nothing really changed despite the advance of commerce brought on through world trade and the industrial revolution. The world was becoming smaller with more people on the move, carrying larger sums. In addition, no longer were companies confined to one spot but were opening many branches in many towns, requiring payrolls to be transported and as such, made them a prime target for thieves.

Only in 1871 did things advance, and it was a giant leap into the modern era.

Using the telegraph, Western Union cleverly created a system of codes that could travel down the telegraph wire. Secure, faster and thrifty, not only did it save time, but cut crime and labour as it travelled sometimes hundreds of miles away.

The next transformation wasn't for a hundred years after in the nineteen-seventies, with the introduction of the credit cards which could be imprinted for records and the ATM.

Quickly after, in the eighties, heralded the arrival of the magnetic strip where credit cards could be swiped rather than pressed and copied.

The noughties brought with it PayPal so money didn't even need a terminal in a shop at all, but could be transferred through the world wide web, enabling the public to pay each other just using an email address.

And now we are in the midst of another great shift. Just enter any McDonalds and you no longer witness the line of smiling faces perched behind a row of tills on a sparkling clean counter. Instead, you might find one face behind a single till as McDonalds transforms towards going cashless.

Neither is it just them. The UK is already as divided on *how to pay*, as it was on Brexit. Venture into a modern café and they may refuse your cash. Yet the grocer next-door refuses digital payments! Hop onto a bus and there's a high probability they won't accept cash, but go for a drink in a bar and you could get charged extra for using your card if the bill is under £10!

Over this past decade, the use of cash has halved, and halved again in the decade prior to that.[116]

In 2015, in the UK, digital payments overtook cash for the first time. Just two years later the figure stood at 60%. It will be interesting to see what that figure stands at after the pandemic. There were a total of 13.2 billion debit card payments in 2019.[117] The cashless high street is coming, and neither is the UK alone.

Australia, China and the Netherlands all have seen similar increases; Denmark and South Korea even more. In Sweden, 70% of consumers say they can happily manage without cash and half of all merchants expect to stop accepting cash by 2025.[118]

Less than 20% of transactions on the street are now performed using cash. Whilst in Norway, cash makes for just 6% of purchases by value. But what is driving this – public demand, the banks or state?

Many point the finger of blame at the banks and it isn't hard to see why.

Banks

In June 1967, in Enfield, North London, a rather non-nondescript branch of Barclays was the location of the world's first ATM. Once the bank's clients were past the shock of withdrawing their cash out of a hole in the wall, and counting it suspiciously, they quickly warmed to it, with good reason. No longer were they limited to bank's opening hours anymore; where they had to stand in a queue waiting for a clerk to turn up. Now they could get their cash 24 hours a day, 365 days of the year - even Christmas! A proven success, ATMs rapidly spread to other branches at other banks, then around the world shortly after,[119] while cash clerks slowly faded away and branches steadily decreased.

Today 92% of all £10 notes in circulation are distributed through ATMs. There is even one located on the South Pole. But for how much longer? History is being repeated. Only this time it is also the ATMs turn to disappear, not just bank clerks.

Which, the UK consumer awareness and protection organisation, claims 275 ATMs are disappearing from our streets every month. That was in 2017. The following year it jumped to nearer 400. If this trend continues, by 2028 all will vanish, along with a great many branches. What's more, the charge for using them is rising. Within the first three months of 2019, 1700 ATMs were no longer free to use but charging anywhere from 95p to £1.99 for each withdrawal.

The banks argue these charges are due it being too costly to keep compared to the new POS (Point of Sale) terminals - the electronic device you hold your card or phone up to when using contactless payments. An ATM, they claim, needs trained staff to regularly maintain and top them up, along with the insurance and costs of buying and maintaining a car. A POS terminal needs none of that – if faulty you just get another through the post.

What's more, in the first four months of 2019, no less than nine ATMs were stolen from locations that straddle the Northern Ireland border alone.[120] With a POS terminal, there's nothing to steal, it's plastic.

Yet as cost-effective as POS terminals are, the banks are forgetting something – us!

Having fewer ATMs around affects us, especially those who have difficulty opening a bank account, such as the homeless, those with mental health problems or the elderly and infirm.

The banks claim they have no choice in the matter as they remain under pressure to cut costs, with many still in debt following the financial crisis and are therefore vulnerable if another were to occur.

Besides, they argue, it is not them pushing for this, but the public themselves.

The Public

There's a simple beauty to cash. We can trust it – it's there in your hand and you'll never get hacked.

So why are so many of us opting to pay through our smartphones or plastic?

To start, cash can weigh you down if you're out for a run or cycling? Or who hasn't boarded a bus to find yourself short of change (if they still take it) and you have to beg a stranger or leave, go to a shop and buy something you don't even want, all to get change!

There is also the added risk of being pick-pocketed, having unwittingly flashed your cash in the market. No one will want to steal your smartphone these days – *they're tracked!*

What's more, transferring coins or notes means transferring germs. Remember Covid!

And out of all the hitches and glitches, we shouldn't forget that cash isn't accepted where we are spending more of our time these days – online! According to the IMF, internet transactions in the UK already account for near 20% of retail sales.[121] In 2008 that figure stood at just 5%.[122]

When looked at closely, it's plain to see why the balance is tipping in favour of using your phone. Cleaner, quicker and you never get short-changed. Furthermore, it's digitally recorded, offering a receipt for every transaction. Whereas you know those paper receipts in your hand, they can be cacogenic due to the film that coats the ink.[123] And where do you store them?

Furthermore, they're empowering people to take more control of their money. In August 2016, the UK government gave the go-ahead for nine of its biggest banks to open their doors to the Fin-Tech sector (Financial Technology). This entailed banks handing over their client's data to the Fin-Tech sector on the provision they first gained consent from the account holders themselves. Thanks to that little big bang, today there exist a plethora of mobile apps for every type person.

There are apps for the over-spenders – dividing bills and savings from that of spending, slowly drip-feeding your spending habits to make sure you have enough money until payday.

Apps for the ambitious savers, dividing pence from the pound and putting every odd penny you get on every transaction to transfer into stocks and shares.

Apps that can lump pension-pots together, to de-confuse you, making it easier to understand.

Some apps monitor all electronic transactions before sifting the credit card market on your behalf to locate the best credit card to suit your needs, offering you a cheaper rate and higher rewards.

Other Apps lump all your bank accounts in one, enabling you to categorise your spending habits, so you can monitor and even alert yourself when you're over-budget.

There are Apps to assist you in saving up specifically for your holiday and how to spend it when there.

Apps for those without access to a bank account, helping the homeless and needy.

Others can transfer dollars to euros and euros to rupees.

And apps that can scan products on supermarket shelves, revealing what the product is, where the product came from and which business; how it was reared, grown, mined or manufactured; how, when, and by whom it was delivered; and how long it has been sitting on the shelf before you. If this isn't informing you, what is?

Yet many people don't know about these. Especially the older. But just like the silver surfers who caught on to the power of the internet a little later than digital natives (kids who grow up in the digital world), they will change in time when they realise how going digital can empower them through giving greater control of what their money does, just as many younger people already have.

So, if the public are switching, what is business's preference when it comes to digital payments?

Business

According to the British Retail Consortium, there seems little point to go cashless when it comes to business simply because credit card fees cost 0.49%, equating to three times that of processing the same transaction by cash.

However, things are not quite that simple. Peer past those costs and factor in the time, labour and security involved in using cash and quite a different picture emerges.

Take the humble cash-register – the frontline for many businesses. Think of the time it takes a person to operate day in, day out. A cashier has to constantly be vigil over a till to make sure no one drops their slippery fingers in.

It can also take a long time for a customer to pull her purse from her bag, count the coins before handing it over. Then, on receiving the money, the cashier has to check it, open the tray, count it and sort it into separate compartments, only to repeat the whole process again and again. When you add up all those transactions, there is a good chance of human error, let alone the time it takes.

Now compare that to tapping a button on the electronic till and the customer tapping his card. *Bing!* No one can steal it either. A business saves a lot in labour costs and is a more efficient enterprise. Neither does it stop there...

What of the labour cost of cashing up every night – a digital register has it already done before you lock the door. Even better, it can transfer the data to you as you sit on a park bench or on beach, enabling you to track your business throughout the day.

There are the banking fees - the time taken to get to the bank and to pick-up or drop-off the cash - time is money in business.

And what about the security risk each time you perform this? The risk of overnight break-ins at the premises or cash going missing from the till – *was it stolen or a genuine mistake?*

Just like the apps for individuals, there is a rich and growing market for cloud-based software when it comes to accounting. Promoted by the likes of Sage, Xero, Quickbooks, most businesses have been quick to recognise how cloud-based software frees up a lot of valuable man-hours. Before this, data stored on location would need support and maintenance contracts, which need to be regularly replaced every four or five years. Besides, what if your premises were to go up in flames!?

Cloud-based data eradicates these problems and takes little to install. It can be accessed anywhere in the world with a connection, have multiple users and present a clear overview of your financial position *on the go,* and be updated *instantly.* An entrepreneur can be on a beach sipping a margarita, knowing exactly how the business is trading there and then. Complex bookkeeping has been made easy – automatic banking feeds, expenses and invoice scanning, auto entering etc. Businesses can now save thousands in accounting fees, working out sums in *zap!* Where it used to take minutes, hours, days!

These are the factors why cash in today's society makes little sense *business-wise.*

It is correct to assume therefore, that it is not the banks, business or even the public pushing for a cashless society, but technology pulling them. So, where is the state's position in all this?

The State

In developed countries, cash accounts for 0.5% of an entire countries GDP. [124] And out of the many ways to perform transactions, cash is the costliest.[125]

There are costs to using the materials that coins and banknotes consist of. They have to be mined or hewn. There is the forging, pulping, pressing and printing; the service costs by way of the designing, counting, storing and distribution. Creating money costs money. There's the environmental damage too – the printing, dying, forging, logistics etc. Not good when we're pressing to go green.

What's more, the finished product can cost more than the sum it represents. It costs eight cents to produce a nickel (five cents). [126] The same can be said of the one-cent piece. Some countries, recognising the ridiculousness of the situation are already scrapping the low denominators – South Korea is even phasing out the use of coins altogether. While the EU went the other way and withdrew the €500 note – not on account of costs but for their excessive use by criminals. Bills in high denominations makes it easy to stash the cash outside of banks.

In addition to the costs involved in producing money, there are costs involved in holding it.

People are less likely to get mugged or pick-pocketed on the street as thieves can't spend your money unless they have your password or fingerprints or face! And with less crime you need fewer police and fewer prisons to maintain, which can prove costly to the taxpayer.

The United States suffered 5,086 bank robberies in 2011.[127] The total sum looted amounted to $38 million. Of the 6,000 people involved, 3,263 were identified and sentenced. It cost a lot of police-time to find them, and it costs a lot to train the police. What is more, once you have the criminals, there's the cost to house them, feed them and prepare them for returning to society.

Another considerable cost is what's referred to as the *grey economy*.[128] This sector has swelled in size in the UK with more people becoming self-employed, choosing to set-up business by themselves (helped immensely by the wireless technology in their pocket). A good thing in itself, yet a high proportion of the transactions undertaken are paid *cash-in-hand*, making it easy for tax-evasion.

It is clear that the positive effects combined outweigh the shortfalls, and as such, the UK government is committed to investing over a billion pounds 'to transform HMRC (Her Majesty's Department of Revenues and Customs) into one of the most digitally advanced tax administrations in the world.' From April 2019, all VAT registered businesses have been obliged to pay VAT digitally. This requires every VAT registered business to:

- Record transactions in digital form
- Preserve those records for up to 6 years
- Create a VAT return from these records
- Submit info to the tax authorities digitally using compatible software

However, they have some catching up to do - Norway and New Zealand are already ahead in this game.

Calculating the Varied Rates

Processing tax returns digitally creates one seamless trail showing (a) the VAT registration numbers, (b) where the transaction took place, (c) between which two parties and (d) the *rate of VAT*. Which all brings us back to, variable VAT rates.

Performing everyday transactions *digitally* on the street eliminates the biggest obstacle in adopting a varying rate of VAT – the impracticality of working out such varied calculations.

Furthermore, money being digitalised eradicates the millstone of the extra cost in labour of working them out, as there is no reason, principally or practically, why the software in a POS terminal or PC cannot be reconfigured to calculate variable rates of tax on recognising both the signature of the purchaser and vendor, as it already does today.

Therefore, if variable rates were adopted, any business disinclined to pursue digitised transactions, will not only find it tediously time-consuming and costly to calculate the VAT manually, but because it is in the interest of all businesses to claim back their VAT, using cash goes against the number one rule of business – profit! As it will erode a substantial part, and therefore, offers a gateway for business to adopt the policy.

Moreover, this represents just the start of digitalisation. A public hyperledger goes further. On each digital coin, is one long, virtual trail of every transaction that ever took place. Not only does this provide a perfect record of account - declaring who participated in the exchange - but being open and publicly accessible, a much greater degree of transparency is had, allowing the public to trace the credit history of companies and crucially *the product history too.* The last example of an app on the previous chapter is testament to this. Called *Provenance*, it traces supply chains in food production through a hyperledger, aiming to create:

> '*a new level of trust and quality management into agricultural supply chains, by bringing farmers, logistics companies and distributors together on a blockchain platform driven by autonomous IoT measurements. By identifying, measuring and analyzing supply chain blind spots, T-Provenance enables new levels of quality assurance, waste reduction and supply chain efficiency gains.*' *And...*
> '*The trust Provenance blockchain platforms (agnostic for produce type i.e., fruit, veg, meat, wine, seafood etc) creates the trust environment for date integration and information exchange, allowing each participant in the supply chain to prove their role in the handling of the food product.*'

Because '*smart contracts*' are performed digitally through a hyperledger, once performed, they can never be changed, leaving an immutable trail of information that flows between users and is permanently open to the public. This makes clear when and where the product came from (food in this case), who delivered it and how. Thus, on tracking business transactions, we are able to trace a product right back to its source, providing a giant step in advancing our knowledge of the marketplace and helping to do away with the veil business has been hiding behind for too long. Thus, digitalising money, not only empowers consumers by informing when and what they are investing in, but the state too, and having this knowledge at our fingertips, we can test and trace businesses on their individual sustainable footprints, and as such, tax them in accordance to that.

Again, money is changing, and so just as we learnt to recognise coins were better than salt, the telegraph better than banknotes, going digital gifts us the ability to transform businesses and industries away from exploiting our environment, to exploiting the Age of Information instead.

9. THE DIVISION OF COMPETITION & PRINCIPLES

The Six Channels

The tools a capitalist traditionally employs to create a product have hardly changed. To develop goods and services, they must *source* materials/information to take to their *premises*, whereby they *process* them into their unique products. Once this *product* is made, it is then *packaged* before being *distributed* to where it is sold.

1) Sourcing
2) Premises
3) Processing
4) Product/Service
5) Packaging
6) Distribution

Of course, the tools – or channels – differ from industry to industry and business to business. Sometimes all are used and at other times, few. By introducing *'sustainability'* as a further channel which can uniquely overlap the others, it enables capitalists to directly outgrow their competitors by profiting more through contributing less tax and growing their brands, while reducing their prices. However, like any competition, rules and divisions must be applied to make it fair and open.

Take a high-tech, heavy industry such as automobile manufacturing. It goes through a much more protracted and rigorous production process than, say a company specialising in antivirus software. Comparing the environmental damage in purchasing a car over computer software may in principle be a good thing, but it brings with it all sorts of scary scenarios. Besides, Neo-Eco-liberalism does not seek to elevate all life above human liberty to create some Ecotopian state, but double-lock sustainability into the business agenda, until the time *may come* when the menace of climate change has abated and ecological breakdown has been reversed. As such, a different set of divisions must be drawn.

The most obvious of which is to ring-fence *industries*. Not only does it make it easier for the State to monitor, but enables businesses to learn from one another, providing an easier target to aim for and comprehend.

Pursuing this, enables each sector to have the VAT rate varied upon the weight of use for each channel within that chosen sector.

So, a tavern, for example, has to source its spirits, ciders and ales, its energy, glasses and food, just as a manufacturer of toasters has to for sheet-metals and plastics. Whereas an insurance provider does little sourcing as it creates what are intangible assets. However, both have premises to operate and a greater disparity in the VAT should therefore be placed on the premises of the insurer than its other channels, whereas a tavern should have a greater disparity in VAT focused on sourcing, premises and products, then processing, packaging and distribution. While a bicycle manufacturer should have the VAT more evenly spread out over all six channels.

However, to better help explain the model, for now, imagine we were to quash the universal VAT rate of 20% and replace it with a variable rate of 4% on each of the six channels at this stage (sourcing, premises, processing, the product, packaging & distribution) thereby making a variable rate of 0 – 24%.

Economies of Scale

The second division would be that of size. A single cafe operated by two staff and clearing £45,000 per annum is little match for a chain consisting of 2,000 staff and reaping over £40 million. The larger player, in all probability, would not only be in a better position to employ more specialists and have a richer knowledge because of it, but would be able to attract higher capital to secure local sources at lower prices too.

For these reasons, it would be unfair to set the same targets for tax reduction regardless of size. Which leads us to question what is the right way to measure a company? By the number of employees or assets? Perhaps sales or just plain old profit? After all, if a company is making no money, how can it invest?

Taking profit first, the downside here is many businesses registered on the stock market are hyped in value (growth stocks) before they have yet to make a single cent of profit. This is due to investors believing those businesses are set to grow quicker, offering them a greater rate of return in the future. Tesla's shares rose 700% in 2020 alone, valuing it at $500 billion, making it the most valuable car company in the world, worth more than General Motors, Ford, Fiat Chrysler and Toyota combined. Yet all it made was just $721 million in profit, compared to the $6 billion just Toyota made by itself.

Another contention is corporations are known to purposefully reduce their profit margins by raising dividend payments, bonuses and executive pay, as this enables them to win both ways. Indeed, it is not uncommon to even hand out loans at meagre rates to shareholders as it has a knock-on effect of reducing the business's income, so they pay less tax (remember Thames Water). As such, using the metric of 'profit' gifts these firms an unfair advantage.

Another indicator of size would be the *number of employees.* Let's not even go there as it would encourage redundancies.

Another factor would be *Market valuation,* though this is far from ideal too, as companies can gain or lose huge valuations in a single day, making it far too volatile. Apple had $64 billion knocked off its share price on a single day, on the announcement of one its chip suppliers have difficulty.

Out of all the metrics that could be used, the most suitable would be *assets.* Not only is it a good indicator of size, giving an indication of its ability to invest in changing its practice and leveraging that advantage over other competitors; but it directly deals with one of the chief criticisms of the current state of the western economy – the ballooning of the financial industry. Following the decades of low interest rates, the deregulation of the financial industry and quantitative easing programmes that were put in place to stabilise the market after the financial crash and covid pandemic, investors gravitated towards pumping money into fixed assets such as property, as opposed to innovating, helping to create a rent-seeking economy.[129] This has caused the industry to become artificially inflated to the point where a house is no longer a home, or a workshop a workspace, but seen as *an asset,* providing a fixed source of income that investors sit on and wait for the price to rise, while the public further down the pay-scale and entrepreneurs starting up, have ever-increasing expenses, including heating, making it harder for them to function.

Using this metric would at least encourage businesses to sell-off property, unblocking a bottleneck in the economy, enabling people and entrepreneurs who are wanting to move on, while encouraging those who hold property to transform them sustainably, or to switch and invest in industry - no bad thing. In the US for example, buildings account for 39% of all carbon emissions.[130] Be that as it may, neither would assets alone act as a fair measure of size, as many older businesses are already struggling to survive. Besides, assets may be inflated artificially now in North America, the UK and antipodean states, but what's to say it will be like that in the future?

A better solution would be to follow the example used by the *Forbes 500,* basing their results not on any single factor, but four points – sales, profits, assets and market value. Not ideal, for this is the hardest challenge I can see to Neo-ECO-liberalism being realised, but by broadly setting these divisions it offers the most pragmatic way forward.

Accountability

Today, it is not rare for executives to perform immoral deeds only for them to walk away with complete impunity. Neo-Eco-Liberalism seeks to change this on a number of levels.

To start, it will be harder to cross the moral line from the outset, given it actively *encourages* companies to avoid tax.

Secondly, in adopting digital payments it makes it much harder for fraudsters as the transaction has been digitally recorded, leaving a long electronic trail that can be accessed remotely. Not only does it simplify the investigations into any wrongdoing, but being etched on a public ledger, it can be traced back at any time – thus making any chicanery impossible to sweep under the carpet.

Furthermore, on cheating being committed, penalties could and should be carried out against that company in the form of escalating the tax and lowering the rating of the eco-label, commensurate upon the context of the offence committed.

Neither should the penalty be placed solely on the business but the executive of that company – whether they remain affiliated or not.

Finally, on NEL being adopted in more than one state and one was found to house corporations that repeatedly violated the rules, other companies based within that state should be marked down, but at a lesser rate, ensuring the government responsible for monitoring sustainability does not favour its native businesses.

Diversification

An artificial enterprise is every bit a prisoner of its environment as the living. As such, when NEL is realised, certain businesses will find themselves at an advantage over others in being more environmentally and sustainably friendly - be it their own making or luck. Either way, the more numerous and varied the options to reduce VAT, the more level the playing field while the greater our chances of avoiding any one of the tipping points.

Take a coffee roasting company located in a rural community, odds are it would score lower on distribution than one located in the city. However, other avenues would exist for it to win back the advantage. Being rural puts it in a better position to enhance biodiversity. It could replace its wall with a hedge of native flora, transferring the bricks to the nearest aggregate company to break down or recycle, thus saving the latter business the action of extracting raw natural resources. It could collect the used coffee grounds upon delivering the fresh coffee and recycle it through commercial gardeners/mushroom farmers or transform the used-grinds into fuel pellets. It could find itself in an area that leads to flooding and make its carpark water-retentive; install a greywater recycling system or convert its roof to 'deep green' – all of which saves taxpayer money being washed away.

The more opportunities for a business to reduce VAT, the more ways the capitalist will innovate new methods to mitigate the effects of climate change, making the market more effective than any government.

Participation

The planetary crisis and business are interconnected. Every business is affected by its climate and landscape as much as it affects them. On opening pollution and waste to the market through competition, it is only fitting that every business is given the opportunity to do their bit and not be excluded from the scheme. Today however, specific sectors are exempt from paying VAT to HMRC (The UK tax authority) [131] – antique dealers, betting shops, banks, amongst others. Therefore, despite corporation tax not being subjected to the same level of scrutiny as VAT – as it is not linked directly to the public – it is only correct to make those industries beholden to a variable corporation tax and based upon the same standards of sufficiency and using the same label.

Transparency

By making the rate of VAT contingent upon the environmental standard of the business, competition will inevitably increase. This *acceleration of capitalism* therefore requires greater transparency, and thus it is essential for companies to display their rating through a universal design that is quick and easy to comprehend through using colour, shapes numbers and such like.

- It must be made clear on the packaging, alongside the brand and proportionate to its size.

- It must display on its website the eco-label.

- Along with a history of its ratings.

- And the QR Code, revealing the traceability of the product.

Having such policies in place allows for the exchange of ideas to flourish, which cannot be overlooked, as it was a key ingredient at the earlier stages of the industrial revolution. Thus, any individual or business will be able to question the results, thereby limiting the chances for *bad* tax avoidance, whilst allowing other businesses to learn what they could be doing wrong - or right – presenting a wider opportunity to take action, thus increasing our chances of avoiding any one of the tipping points.

What's more, being *online* also makes it easier for the state to monitor, as it can double-check the link between companies and their suppliers, locating anomalies.

A business must also be open to random inspections with the minimum of notice.

In addition, in light of the 'big four' global auditing firms falling wide of the mark in terms of their accounting practices, inspectors need to be rotated on a biannual basis, to reduce the chances of inspectors getting *too close* to business.

Moreover, making the rate of VAT dependent on environmental standards offers the potential to break what has long been the bane of neoliberalist values – *patents*.

Patents

Patents were devised to reward inventors for the sum of their efforts, and drive progress. Yet they perform the exact opposite by creating monopolies, thus blocking innovation and widening utility.

A prime example is the Wright Brothers. Despite being feted as the early pioneers of flight, most of the early innovations did not come from them but their competitors. Indeed, the infamous brothers were without doubt the first to record a successfully controlled flight. However, it is well documented in the legal records how much of their time was spent defending their patents. One of those they repeatedly dragged through the courts was Glenn Curtiss, the inventor of the 'Aileron' or 'horizontal rudder' - *which they later used*. Curtiss, on the other hand, innovated publicly without concern. The result of this, was the US aeroplane industry remained stagnant until World War I erupted, by which time the German aeroplanes – not subjected to patents – were far superior.

Despite this lesson, some say history is repeating itself, for in China much of the technical wizardry is open-source, enabling entrepreneurs to freely use each other's innovations. Whereas in the West, patents generally permit a twenty-year monopoly. To block the spread of green technology at a time when we're racing against the clock, defies reason.

NEL proposes to do away with patents and reward designers by allowing businesses to make deeper cuts in VAT and/or over extended periods in proportion to the improved sustainability the designer's product will make. This will enable independent inventors to auction off their technology to business, rewarding value to both parties. While on a business developing new technology will not hold a monopoly through their patents, but offered a reduced rate of VAT.

10. QUANTIFYING BUSINESS SUSTAINABILITY

The Circular Economy

In 1962 a book titled *Silent Spring* was published. Its author, Rachel Carson, describes both scientifically and eloquently the food cycle that exists on Earth; how it took hundreds of millions of years to reach, passing from one species to the next. However, this cycle of life that we are part of, has been broken through the extensive use of pesticides. They lie in the soil, infiltrating organisms and passing from one to the next – creating a chain of poisoning and death.

Despite the chemical industry refuting her accusations and wanting the book banned, sales of her book surged. One-hundred and fifty thousand copies were published on its first print run alone, having a huge impact upon the environmental movement. Moreover, it successfully brought changes to the legal use of pesticides.

Amongst her admirers was Kenneth Boulding, an economist who saw the blame should not lie solely with the chemical industry, but the economic framework that allowed for it; how raw materials were extracted without consideration for the flora and fauna and then transported from one side of the planet to the other, for being a fraction cheaper than using materials closer to home; how they were processed into products that were designed to fall apart, so consumers will consume yet more; and how products at the end of their lives are left to waste, releasing toxins into the soil, water and food chain.

Seeing how our economy was designed with little consideration for the natural world, he published what was the first concept of a *circular economy* in 1966. Essentially, his idea focused upon shifting from a 'cowboy' economy, where we view the world as an open frontier that we take for granted, and move towards a 'spaceman' economy, where we recognise and adapt to what this planet can provide.

Since then, the concept has been refined many times to contain several schools of thought. Though varied, all take a holistic approach to capitalism and explain the practical ways a business can do their bit for the natural environment by way of:

a) Reducing our carbon footprint.

b) Reducing material consumption.

c) Reducing the use of harmful chemicals.

d) Making goods more serviceable and durable.

e) Designing products to separate into reusable components.

f) Reusing the materials in products when reaching the end of their shelf life.

g) Designing products to be modular/used for several purposes, thus minimising materials and maximising usage.

h) Designing products to enrich biodiversity.

i) Recycling materials through one of two loops – the *technical* or *biological.*

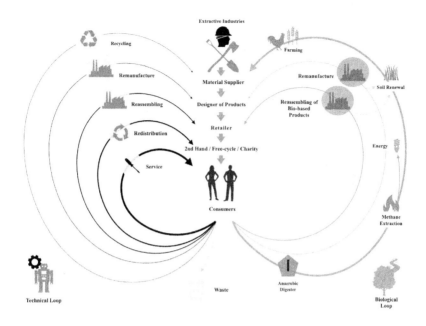

The biological loop (on the right) performs this by designing all goods to consist of biodegradable substances, thus allowing those goods to break down naturally into the environment without adverse effects.

While the technical loop (on the left), in recognising the need to have products made of artificial materials, aims to stop waste by making goods super-durable, reusable or recyclable.

The shorter and thicker the line in the loop, the better, as less energy and materials are consumed.

Despite the case for a circular economy being accepted since the 1960s, industries have failed to make the jump due to there being no financial incentive.

Digital payments make this feasible by enabling the universal rate of VAT to change from business to business, as it takes away the complex issue of having to calculate the rates, crucially permitting us to pin the rate to the sustainability targets A to I.

Businesses can achieve this through improving their sustainability along the six channels:

1) Sourcing   2) Premises

3) Processing   4) Product/Service

5) Packaging   6) Distribution

When a business creates goods, at every step of the way, energy and materials are used which emit by-products.

Sourcing, for example, tends to be a logistical operation, dealing with supply and procurement along with maintenance, which at its very least, produces carbon dioxide. Shipping is the beating heart of globalisation but burns through two billion barrels of crude oil. Added to which, the ships themselves are full of harmful toxins that are rarely recycled properly and leak into the environment.

On the other hand, the *premises* of certain service businesses can consume more energy than all other channels.

As for the *production process*, apparatus today are higher up the scale of efficiency than a decade ago, yet companies often gain more profit from advertising than investing in machinery and selling off their old apparatus to developing nations.

Products are often designed to stall or completely fail within a given period.

Packaging is a significant factor in contributing to marine pollution and landfill sites.

And in *distribution*, goods are often manufactured on one side of the globe from where it is to be sold, simply due to labour being a fraction cheaper.

On top of this, inspections need to be undertaken and none is more important than the start.

Domesday 2.0

In 1085, England was under threat from invasion. To know how much tax the king could raise to fund an army, he undertook what was the most thorough survey of any country at the time – the great *Domesday book*. So detailed was it, that it was likened to the day of judgment or 'Domesday,' when Christians believed everybody would be judged before God.

Covering much of England and Wales, the book extended over 913 pages and registered over 13,000 places, including every farm. One Anglo-Saxon chronicle said of it, *'So very narrowly did he have it investigated that there was no single hide nor yard of land, nor indeed… one ox or cow or pig which was left out and not put down in his record.'*

Like then, again we are under threat and need to balance the tax correctly. Thus, what we need is another 'Domesday', a modern way. To inspect the natural landscape every business is located in, every factory, plant and warehouse, the machinery and appliances the business operates, along with the energy it consumes, the materials it sources and who and where they redistribute to, along with their waste.

Once this data is collated, it should be input into a hyperledger accessible and open to all, so businesses can learn from one another and improve their prospects, and ours.

Assessing the Six Channels

What I suggest in the following, is not a fixed template but more a starting block, showing what businesses can do to mitigate the ecological breakdown we are causing and more crucially for them, *reducing their VAT*. And once capitalists realise how to profit from the prevention of climate change, they will be scheming up ever new ways, and the examples I present will become archaic, as they refine their research, practices and goods.

1. Sourcing

The extraction of raw materials is responsible for up to 90% of our biodiversity disappearing. Yet rather than slowing it down, its increasing - threefold since the 1970s.

Decimating the natural landscape to be but a link in the production chain also accounts for 53% of the world's carbon emissions. Despite this shocking statistic, few businesses take it into account when sourcing materials, which, when looked at through the eyes of a purchaser, is not surprising.

- What is the rating on the eco-label?
- Local, national, international or from non-NEL states?
- Transported by air, road or sea?
- What is the efficiency and engine type – electric, hydrogen, petrol or diesel?
- If shipped, are sails used at any time or solar to assist its passage?

2. Premises

In 2019, annual greenhouse gas emissions were almost sixty billion tonnes of CO_2 equivalent, and growing. Together, buildings and their construction are responsible for around 39% of all carbon emissions, with operational emissions (the energy used to adjust the temperature and lighting of buildings) accounting for 28%. The remaining 11% comes from embodied emissions or 'upfront' carbon associated with materials and construction processes throughout the entire life of the of building.[132]

To add to this, buildings consume vast amounts of energy and water, along with materials. Despite knowing this, for years too little is being done as buildings continue to be erected that waste huge amounts of CO_2. There exist thousands of ways corporations can do their bit to reduce their VAT, whether via retrofitting existing buildings or through the erection of new premises. Both of which can be divided into five categories – design, materials (and the energy they consume), waste, water treatment, and the impact of the building upon the local habitat.

2.1. Design

Whether in an existing building or designing one anew, a business can adapt to become as energy efficient as a Passivhaus,[133] where little or no energy is used from the public power grid as it generates energy itself, exporting what excess it has.

- What is the overall 'U' value of the building? (the level of heat it retains)

- Insulation – natural, recyclates, artificial.[134]

- The glazing – are they double or triple glazed. What of its thickness? (windows can now harness solar power or be designed to reflect the sun in harsh, hot climates). What direction are the windows positioned? And in a colder climate, are they angled to face the sun? If the temperature rises too high in summer or cold in winter, having a canopy above will block out the sun when it climbs high at midday to block it. However, come winter, when the sun remains lower over the horizon, it can continue to penetrate through the glass from dawn till dusk.

- Deciduous trees represent an even better way. Placing them between the windows and the sun, they can partially block the sun in summer, preventing the interior from overheating. Yet in winter, having shed their leaves, sunlight shines through to warm the cold interior. They also provide a welcome habitat for wildlife, enhancing biodiversity, can act as a windbreak, block noise, stabilise water tables and promote mental health, as numerous studies prove.

- The roof? Is it living – not only can they absorb heat, providing an excellent form of insulation, but they can also stop UV damage. What type is it – one for succulents, bushes or trees?

- Is the building modular – can it be added to/taken apart to be used on other sites, extending the life of the building's materials.

- Does the design encourage people to use the stairs more, rather than take the elevators/escalators?

- Can the building/production process be shared with other corporations, saving space and production equipment?

- What lighting is used to save energy?

- Is the building designed to fuse with the landscape and help it thrive?

If the design and location of the building has taken all this into account, what of the materials?

2.2. Materials

In the current business environment, there exists a vast array of materials to choose from. Corporations opt for which materials to use based upon their physical, chemical and tactual properties, along with the usual factors like cost and availability etc. However, NEL opens up other factors that allow companies to profit.

- Are the materials locally available?

- Are they reclaimed from recycled materials or recyclates? (goods that are partially recycled)

- How hazardous are the materials to the people, flora and fauna around the building, and globally?

- Are they sustainable?

- What is the embodied cost?

The purpose of focusing on design and materials is essentially to reduce energy, thereby reducing our emissions. For once a single foreign particle enters the environment, it causes harm and not just for the planet. It feeds flash floods, hurricanes and droughts. According to a Harvard study conducted in 1995, one hundred thousand people in the US alone die every year on account of airborne particles.[135]

2.3. Energy

- What is the volume of energy used in proportion to its size compared to its sector?

- Does it use active solar energy or photovoltaic cells, or the photovoltaic-thermal type?

- Are wind turbines installed?

- Does it recycle the heat from its computers, the pathways people walk on, roads or windows?

- Does it use solar thermal water heaters?

- Are trigeneration systems employed, i.e., is it able to produce electricity and alter the temperature itself?

- Does it have ground source heat pumps installed?

- Does it employ the use of heat exchangers?

- Does it have solar chimneys for passive ventilation and light?

- What about Bio-mass boilers to generate energy?

- Bio-fuel generation to use waste cooking oil?

- Does it tap into hydropower?

With **design, materials** and **energy** being allowed to influence a company's VAT rate, significant reductions can be had by retrofitting existing buildings.[136]

2.4. Water

Between California and Hawaii, floating in the vast Pacific Ocean, an enormous patch of waste exists that is equal in size to continental Europe,[137] and it's growing.

It is believed 46 million pieces of plastic per sq. mile circle our oceans – six times more plastic than that of plankton!

One hundred thousand marine animals and a million seabirds die every year through ingesting plastic. In 2005 a piece of plastic found in an albatross stomach bore a serial number tracing it to a World War II seaplane shot down in 1944. Computer models re-creating the plastic's journey showed it to have spent a decade floating in the sea just South of Japan before drifting slowly 6,000 miles to an area of America's West Coast where it continued to float, circling for the next fifty years.[138]

The Pacific Ocean is but one part of the puzzle, fed from the rubbish of China, Indonesia, Malaysia, Vietnam et al. Along the British coastline, around the upper part of the North Sea, for every 100-metre stretch, there are 900 pieces of trash. According to GESAMP (The UN department that deals with marine pollution), 80% of the waste in our seas is estimated to come from land-based sources. So what is all this to do with business premises? A lot.

When a storm occurs, water hits the roofs, roads and pavements, causing water levels to rise. As it does, it picks up all the trash and waste on our streets, roads and fields before it gets washed down our drains, ditches, streams and rivers, where it makes its way out to sea.

But by reducing the flow of water from our roofs and streets it will help to limit the chances of floods and the trash that gets washed out to sea. As such, by analysing the flow of water and rating its quality before and after it leaves the premises, it will help to improve our water quality.

- Does the premises harvest rainwater?
- Does it use greywater recycling to irrigate its grounds?
- Does it use reed filtrations for wastewater, filtering out the impurities and lessening the pressure on the wider waterways?
- Does the carpark soak up rain rather than discharge it straight down the drain?
- If using cement, what type and can it absorb water?
- Does it have a green, living roof – not only does this insulate the building but holds up to 70% of the water that hits its surface, significantly limiting the storm-water runoff?
- Are its walls living, helping to soak up/retain the water longer, increasing the local biodiversity?
- Does the building contain water-efficient devices such as aerated, push or proximity detection taps?
- The restrooms, are they fitted with dual-flush?
- Is the wastewater from the basins reused to fill the cisterns?
- Does the WC use a composting system, returning waste to the soil?

2.5. *The local habitat*

With the urban environment perpetually creeping into what wildlife refuges are left, our responsibility is to limit, stop, then reverse this trend. Business can have a large hand in this, for they can help create the living bridges and pathways that lure nature back.

- Are the land boundaries of the business suitable for wildlife?
- Are there tunnels underneath the highway creating a corridor for wildlife?
- Again, are its walls or the roof living using native local flora?
- Does it link the premises to cycleways?
- Does it have cycle lockups?
- Are its carparks living, breathing spaces?
- Does the carpark display & guide you to the spaces available, saving unnecessary emissions?
- Are charging points available for electric vehicles?
- Does it protect native wildlife? It will score for what flora and fauna are found – both their numbers and diversity, compared to the vicinity outside the premises.
- Does it have a reed filtration bed – an excellent habitat for birds and pond life, something that has shrunk the world over.
- How environmentally friendly are the façades of the building? Are they non-hazardous to flora and fauna, insect-friendly and have nesting sites?

An excellent example of this in the UK is Angel Square, Manchester. Headquarters for the Co-Operative Group, it is one of the most sustainable buildings in Europe. Achieving a score of 95.32% from BREEAM (Building Research Establishment Environmental Assessment Method). Positioned to maximise passive solar gain, it reduces the need for heat. It both harvests rainwater and recycles its greywater. It also embraces waste heat recycling, using an adiabatic process and has a double skin façade.[139]

3. Processing

It is the production process that is most responsible for the toxification of the environment and continues to increase. Heavy industry tends to go through a prolonged process, even requiring them to become the size of a small town. Whereas a service industry, such as a garage mechanic, dry cleaners or bank, will be a much simpler process.

- What pollutants are emitted and are these Airborne, waterborne or solids?
- How much water is consumed and what is the quality on exiting the facility compared to entering?
- Does it recycle wastewater on-site?
- Does it employ a carbon capture scheme?
- How much energy does the processing use?
- Is the process insulated and/or able to transfer the heat to other areas in need, lessening its draw on the power grid?
- Can it transform waste into energy to use at its premises or that of another?

Many businesses show an unwillingness to adapt because there has never been the need – why change what goes on when sources remain cheap, reliable and the customer never questions?

Because of this, many companies don't know nor want to know what chemicals go into producing their goods, let alone the harm they cause. Exposing and correcting this has long been the task of government, only it has a poor record of being slow to act - not helped of course by corporate lobbyists or the turnover of those in office. But given the incentive to change, it would make for a different story.

An example of what can be done is the case highlighted in the book 'Cradle to Cradle,' by William McDonagh's and Michael Braungart, whereby they transformed a Swiss textile mill awash with pollutants into a clean, efficient production process, eliminating all harmful toxins. If a textile manufacturer can perform this (one of the most polluting industries) with little financial incentive, it leaves little to the imagination what the industry can do if money is involved.

4. The Product

If but one channel could be changed, the most far-reaching would be the product itself.

If you stop waste, you would only find more products coming off the production line.

If you stop sourcing materials, people would only need more goods.

If you were to turn every building to a Passivhaus standard, products will continually be designed around breaking and polluting. Changing the design of the product to last longer and using fewer resources, changes everything. Pursuing this course enables the landscape to stay largely intact, for there will be less transport on the roads, less packaging and waste, which altogether makes for a more sustainable world.

Somewhere back, this common-sense approach got washed away by our faith in *growth fixes everything!* Nowhere is this better expressed than in the Ealing comedy film: 'The Man in the White Suit.' It goes something like this…

One day, a chemist working for a textile mill creates a new wonder material that shines in the dark, never gets dirty and never, ever wears. The factory owner, excited, puts the wonder material into production. Rubbing his hands, he knows he has hit the jackpot and is able to quash all his competitors, monopolising the entire textile industry! As the machinery starts to churn, an anxiety creeps into the town – not only will it be the end of all the other mills, but the mill that makes it, for once everyone buys their suit, trousers or skirts etc, in this material, they will never have to buy clothes again. Then people in the town will lose their jobs, as will the shops that the mills support! Soon anxiety turns to panic and the entire town is out with pitchforks in the night hunting down the man in the white suit (the Chemist) and his bid to revolutionise this industry.

This fictional comedy represents the financial strategy our economy has adopted and shaped us culturally – how we live to work to spend, as opposed to work to live.

- Are the materials non-hazardous/toxic?

- Is it designed to be easily serviced?

- Is it designed with universal fittings, so one tool suits all – not their exclusive tool that you have to buy only for the design to be out of date shortly after?

- Are the materials derived from the biological loop and harmless for the environment?

- Or is the design made to fit the technical loop?

- Does it use reclaimed/recyclable materials rather than raw resources?

- Is it designed to embrace locally grown or manufactured materials?

- Is it of a modular design that can be added to or upgraded easily?

- Is it designed so individual parts can be replaced rather than the product as one and easily disassembled, remanufactured or recycled?

- Is it designed for ease of transport, saving emissions and space?

- Is it designed to be put together by the purchaser?

5. Packaging

The problem of waste is a simple one – it's a material we generate that no one wants to keep, and packaging is responsible for much of that, generating a high demand on the plastics industry which is derived from fossil fuels.

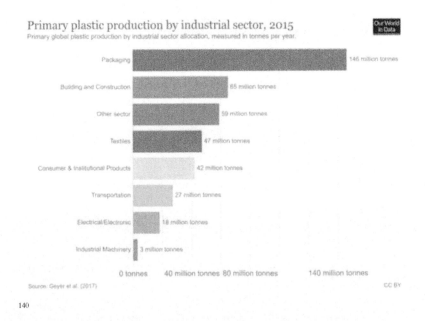

Primary plastic production by industrial sector, 2015

Primary global plastic production by industrial sector allocation, measured in tonnes per year.

Packaging	146 million tonnes
Building and Construction	65 million tonnes
Other sector	59 million tonnes
Textiles	47 million tonnes
Consumer & Institutional Products	42 million tonnes
Transportation	27 million tonnes
Electrical/Electronic	18 million tonnes
Industrial Machinery	3 million tonnes

Source: Geyer et al. (2017)   CC BY

140

Enter your nearest supermarket and examine the cereal packets, the boutique biscuit tins or just general 'hardware'. These goods are regularly packaged not just to protect the goods, but provide marketing. A bigger box deceives us into believing we get more for our money while enhancing the chances of being seen, hitting two birds with one stone for business. A government committee once questioned cereal manufacturers on why they produce this unnecessary waste. To which they responded, it was a side effect of the production process - the machines, they claimed, filled the packets at the start of the process and it is only as they make their way along the production line and when entering distribution, that the cereals sink – *really?*

Or visit any fashionable, upmarket boutique, and you may well be handed a big bag displaying their logo despite having the size of goods you bought being very small. This *advertising on the cheap* is because they are not made accountable for the waste they produce needlessly, but society instead, as it is the government that has to pay via the rubbish collections, landfills and incinerators, all of which contribute to the chances of you, your partner or your children catching the particles in their lungs, leading to cancer, asthma and an increased burden on public healthcare, or that is if it hasn't been washed out to sea.

These concerns over the years have slowly been getting addressed through regulations. But this is unfair, costly and proved very time-consuming. If, however, we were to reward those who use the least, backed up by the eco-label, the values of the market will become more aligned with our larger society.

In the EU, 170 kilograms of packaging was generated per person in 2016, ranging from 55 kg in Croatia to 221 kg in Germany. The majority of which consists of paper and cardboard (41%), which you may think is harmless but isn't.

Packaging waste generated by packaging material, EU, 2016
(%)

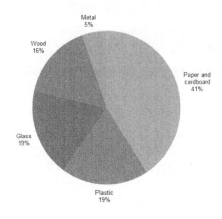

Notes: Data from the EU aggregate have been estimated by Eurostat
Source: Eurostat (env_waspac)

eurostat

Inks in packaging can be toxic. Heavy metals such as: cadmium, chromium, copper, lead, mercury, nickel and zinc, all go into the printing process. In addition, each can vary depending on the colour of the ink used. Red for example, is more toxic than green and green more toxic than blue.[141]

Metal (times)	Blue[1]	Green	Red[2]	Yellow
Cd	+3.25	-0.58	+5.85	+2.5
Cr	+5	+1.85	+3.26	-5.71
Cu	-128	-311	+2.04	-34.14
Pb	-0.66	+2.00	+29.67	+7.2
Hg	-2	+4.31	2.22	-1.51
Ni	-3.75	+1.42	-2.81	-60.8
Zn	+2.34	-15.95	+2.43	0
[1]Reflex blue, [2]Warm red				

There is some good news however, as a higher proportion of materials are being recycled than ever. In 2016 the EU recycled 55%. But beware, recycling concentrates the chemicals in the packaging.

Besides pulp (paper and cardboard), the two other popular materials used are glass and plastic, each representing 19%.

Glass has an advantage over plastics in that it doesn't contain toxins, is easily reused and can be recycled without loss of purity or quality. Its drawbacks are its heaviness and fragility, which make it more suited to short distances. Another being its demand on fossil fuels, which is required to power the furnace that produces the glass.

Plastics on the other hand, are durable, lightweight and cheap, making it ideal, or until that comes to the matter of waste. Soon there will be more plastic in our vast blue oceans than fish. Already 70% of the seafood we consume is estimated to contain traces of plastic, and that's set to last well beyond the life of yourself, your grandchildren and theirs!

A study in July 2020, by Royal Holloway University, revealed that crabs in the river Thames contained plastic in their stomachs, intestines and gills. Many of the fibres were so tightly tangled their stomachs were filled.[142]

Across the Atlantic, in the US, 42% of the rivers tested turned positive to Bisphenol A (BPA), one of the more damaging chemical additives found in plastics.[143] BPA is an endocrine disruptor that acts rather like the female hormone oestrogen. Many scientific studies have brought evidence linking BPA to hormonal changes in both children and adults, linking it to prostate and breast cancer,[144] miscarriages, diabetes and the rise of male infertility.[145] BPA is in food packaging, plastic bottles, canned food and paper receipts (the film that locks in the ink).

Phthalates is another band of chemicals where they are known to have negative health impacts similar to above. Recent research in rats discovered plastic particulates were passed through the placenta into the foetus to lodge into the heart, brain, lungs, liver and kidney.[146] And now research has been carried out and confirm the same for humans.[147]

And when it comes to plastics, one third of its entire production is destined for packaging. Furthermore, much of it is only used once before being discarded. These 'single-use plastics' are used by the food industry for the likes of convenience meals[148] or snacks; food that is sold in bunches rather than loose so we are forced against our will to be 4 instead of 2 etc; hardware products that do need to be protected; or used purely to make checkouts more efficient, so supermarkets tills don't have to be manned and just scanned. These are all examples of how boardroom culture is so focused upon driving up profits and growth, not driving down waste and pollution, hence why we are now losing the race against time.

- Is it transported using zero packaging?

- What packaging material is used?

- What level of toxicity is the packaging?

- Is the packaging collected by the courier/haulage company and returned to the factory/depot from where it was dispatched?

- Is the packaging dispatched to collection points within the locality of the purchaser as opposed to door to door, and do they have a recycling facility there?

- Is there a scheme to incentivise the purchaser to return the packaging or recycle it?

- Is the packaging made from recyclable materials?

- Does the packaging contain instructions where and how to recycle?

- Can the packaging be reused in other ways than just packaging, extending its life? If so, are instructions given for this?

6. Distribution

Like sourcing, just in reverse. How are the goods transported?

- By air, road, rail or sea?

- What engine is used and to what level of efficiency? Is it electric, hydrogen, petrol or diesel?

- If shipped, are sails used at any time, or solar to aid its passage?

- Does it share transport with another business, reducing congestion?

For many company directors reading this, it must feel quite daunting – not just in terms of the sheer number of paths there are to invest in, but how alien it all looks. Yet for the canny capitalist out there, he or she will be reading through the list and swelling with ideas, before envisioning the hundreds of possibilities to profit from the process of 'going green' and putting a new purpose to their life, other than getting rich.

For instance, a flooring retailer could find erecting a set of solar panels on the roof and reducing the water run-off, could be enough to reduce the tax rate. While another entrepreneur on realising the scope of change afoot, might start to diversify his/her business and research new ways they can upcycle what they had considered waste.

And the examples I give of the methods to assess a company's practise and product is but the start. For when one corporation starts others will inevitably follow, inventing ever new practices, processes and products, for that is both the beauty and crudity of capitalism – its sheer endless drive and creativity, for profit.

Monitoring

Company House (the government institution where all UK businesses are registered) states: 'At the end of March 2021 there were 4,716,126 companies on the register.'[149] Of those, 2.72 million were registered for VAT and/or Pay As You Earn (PAYE) in the UK,'[150] by March 2019.'

No small number.

Now add the staff employed at HMRC (the UK tax authority), which in 2021 numbered 66,000.[151] If you were then to divide that figure by the number of companies registered, the figure comes to roughly 41, equating the number of companies each member of staff would have to assess and monitor throughout the year.

If only it were that simple.

To start, VAT is not the only taxing issue for the HMRC. Corporation Tax, Capital Gains Tax, Inheritance Tax. They are also responsible for things like Child Benefit, Tax-Free Childcare, Statutory Pay and Tax Credits. What's more, of those staff working at HMRC, many would not have read a single sheet of the 20,000 pages of the UK tax code.

To add to the challenge, with the giant tax leaks through the likes of the Panama and Paradise Papers, HMRC were vilified by the press and public alike,[152] even though the government had reduced their offices to just thirteen.[153] Which means, now if a business in Inverness requested an inspection, the nearest inspector would be located in Glasgow – 156 miles away!

But it wasn't always like this. Around thirty-five years ago, the number of personnel at HMRC would have brought you closer to ninety thousand.

> *'It ran a strong and vibrant system of local tax offices, with one located in just about every community of any size in the UK' The tax office was engaged in the local network of business. We were taxed by people we might have been to school with, and who were now our neighbours. We knew them, and perhaps just as importantly, they knew us and who the rogues were (including amongst the professionals with whom they had to deal). The system created local confidence, local effectiveness and local intelligence which was targeted at reducing the tax evasion that undermined the local economy.'*[154]

> *The Joy of Tax,* Richard Murphy,
> one of the founders of The Tax Justice Network.

Having local tax offices empowers the community, as local tax offices have a greater awareness of the district. However, returning to this will undoubtedly be an added burden on the taxpayer, for which there are three counterarguments.

Firstly, the primary purpose of a tax office is to raise funds for the government, and as such, reducing their budget acts as a double-edged sword, given it is easier for rogue businesses to escape through the net.

Secondly, switching to a digital economy brings significant savings for the economy – directly and indirectly – counterbalancing the rollout costs of local tax offices.

Thirdly, a tax office is not just a processing machine to help balance budgets. It is a facilitator of social justice and a deliverer of democratic will.

What's more, in any economy, the faster and more fluid the transactions, the faster goods and services evolve and develop, thus accelerating capitalism. However, this noble law in economics runs parallel to one of physics – the more we consume goods in a linear fashion, the more we destroy the environment and atmosphere, on which all life depends. Under the current form of neoliberalism, it doesn't so much as follow the first law, as drags it brazenly while riding roughshod over the second.

NEL seeks to form a synthesis between the two, making the transaction process itself play a pivotal role in protecting the environment, while speeding up the progress in the direction we need. However, to move from a linear to a circular economy and put a halt to any future bottlenecks, a tax office must be properly prepared and fully resilient for any number of businesses putting forward their requests to change their tax rates when they see fit.

This process would have a business filling in an application, stating:

- What change they intend and when?
- What materials they plan to use from which companies?
- What they intend to do with the old machinery/waste?
- What their completion date is?

The tax office would then follow with an assessment. If satisfied with the proposed changes, the office would then request to either pre-inspect the premises or have a representative visit the tax office, along with the enhanced product(s).

Upon receiving the go-ahead for a reduction, the company would make change to its design or business practice.

Once completed, the tax office would be contacted a second time, where they would make a post-inspection. If given the green light, the business would be granted a reduction in VAT and have the changes registered on the ledger.

If any business has not moved forward within a three-year time frame, an inspector will perform a routine check-up on the premises/product to assess it, as it would have to process that data to reset the mean average for the VAT in that sector.

11. RESOLVING THE THREE CRISES

Globalisation and the Public

I'm sitting in a cafe in Edinburgh. Across from me is an elderly couple from Quebec. There is a Spanish barista who is serving me a cappuccino made using Columbian coffee beans. The machine that makes it is Italian. The cup and saucer come from Turkey. The audio speakers are 'Made in China' that happen to be playing songs from Neil Young (US), while the croissants are Scottish, naturally.

Today we live in a truly globalised world. Materials and goods are sourced from various locations, often from different countries, and taken to a manufacturing hub where they are put together prior to being transported across entire oceans for what economists call *comparative advantage*.

David Ricardo first used the term in the early 19th century. Dissecting wine-making in Portugal and the manufacture of cloth in England, he noted how each country is differently endowed and able to produce goods comparatively cheaper than if the other were to import the materials and make the goods themselves.

Much has changed since Ricardo's time. AI and tech have transformed production, as has the internet, which has remodelled office space and the market itself. While today, 60,000 container ships[155] are constantly circling our seas. All this has helped make many businesses become bigger than nation-states, becoming as it were corporatocracies, ceaselessly expanding their market and shifting their practices from one country to the next, in order to gain that narrowest of advantages, and so long as we remain with coins and notes, the environment will remain an externality making the taxpayer continue to pay the brunt of the clean-up, which we know it has a poor record of undertaking.

In 2017, 2% of the United States GDP was wiped out as a result of the wildfires, hurricanes, floods and heatwaves.[156] Now these *extremes* are commonplace, increasing year on year.

Fires raged across the Mediterranean coast in 2021, from Turkey to Portugal. Recognising the millions of dollars the damage caused, and how it is only set to increase, eight nations agreed to collaborate as they could not cope alone.[157]

Global shipping contributes to this. Three percent of global greenhouse gas emissions may seem minor combined to farming or housing, but it's a figure that is set to rise and the shipping industry also happens to be the most polluting.[158]

Ships belch out 'bunker fuel', a tar-like waste product of the oil refining process that is so toxic, few industries use it. One study claimed just two hundred of the world's largest ships produce as much sulphur as all the cars combined, resulting in around 250,000 premature deaths and 6.4 million cases of childhood asthma every year in settlements that straddle the major shipping channels of the world.[159]

Recognising this, in 2020, the International Maritime Organisation (IMO) imposed regulations to cut sulphur emissions. However, as one researcher pointed out, reducing the amount of sulphur will not make the particulates disappear but make them smaller, finer and enter our lungs all the same. The most common-sensical approach therefore, is to reduce shipping. Besides, making goods more local, gives a company a stronger identity within that community, making it act more responsibly.

In having distances over a certain length factored into the VAT and the ECO label, a business considering relocating abroad will weigh the added increase in tax against the lower labour rates, regulations etc.

Therefore, to create the most efficient market and hit a ceiling in emissions quicker, NEL would need to be adopted in more than one state, simply because trading beyond any NEL border would have its lesser green products put at a disadvantage by goods entering from non-NEL-states abroad, given the latter will not be subjected to any mandatory assessment or monitoring process while the former will be taxed heavier than those entering, and the opposite for greener goods.

Thus, for any NEL-state to pursue its green agenda, it would need to levy a duty on goods crossing its border, as odds are, the goods taxed heavier from its own state will be greener than those entering and that's before we take into account the extra distance travelled to get there.[160]

Despite recognising the principles of such a policy, the probability is non-NEL-states would counter such a move by imposing tariffs on the NEL-state's goods entering its borders in turn, declaring the NEL-state to be 'protective' or 'biased' towards its home-grown goods. Yet if the NEL-state were to drop the tariff, it would go back to square one and put half its own goods at an unfair disadvantage, even though their goods that are taxed heavier, will in all likelihood be more sustainable.

One solution is to have those businesses based without, that want to trade within the NEL-bloc, subjected to the same rules as those businesses based within. This would entail them being independently assessed, monitored and randomly opened to checks by private inspectors. Alternatively, the business could set up branches within the NEL-bloc (as happened with many UK moving to the EU, post-Brexit).[161]

Either of these is not a solution in itself, as they come with their own pitfalls. Still, it provides a method to bypass the sticky issue of tariffs and highlights the root of the issue as not technical, but political in nature, as nearly all matters are when pertaining to tax. Indeed, on run up to COP26 in Glasgow, the EU discussed employing something similar, called a 'Carbon Border Adjustment Mechanism,'[162] which the UK trade secretary, Liz Truss happened to back, only to be talked down by much of her party, preferring to harness the, *free market*. With this being the case, along with all the ideas I raise in this book, ultimately it comes down to *you!* No one else. For no matter how much I have come to berate that tiny slither of a thing some call democracy,[163] grasping it, is the only valid means to both reform it, and the economy.

So, the question comes down to, are you happy with the current system and how it's structured? Do you think governments, business and consumers are all doing their best to tackle the planetary crisis? Or do you think we could all be doing more, by profiting from it?

The NEL Solution

With the issue of *globalisation* and *public acceptance* not able to be settled until the day NEL is adopted, of the other challenges, each will have its slew of critics, whether it is the likes of business's believing themselves ill-placed in the wrong division or poorly assessed; investors crying foul, or that of the public fearing hyper-ledgers. Yet as challenging as these are, it's imperative to remind ourselves of the challenges we remain mired in.

Firstly, we are in the midst of an Existential Crisis, fed by the Political Crisis (PC), Economic Crisis (EC) and the Climate Crisis (CB). Each of which is fed by further tributary issues and friction points in our economy.

Advertising (EC) – As individuals, it represents an assault on our *psychological sovereignty,* while at the same time bringing little reward for society. Every year $760 billion is spent on advertising that should be invested in mitigating and preparing for the effects of climate change.[164] In adopting the eco-label, the power of advertising will diminish as it exposes a corporation's truer colours - you can add splendour and pomp to a brand all you like but with the label showing the brand as toxic, fewer and fewer consumers will want to be associated with it, as it will likely cost you more and show you care little for...

Climate Change (EC) (PC) (CB) – Despite the hazard humanity faces, we still rise everyday not to fight this, but for money, which makes us as a species either denialist or a nihilist. Having our values clash with what we practice exposes how our economic system is broken. NEL seeks to correct this by factoring the environment into the price at the point of exchange, essentially merging financial values closer to the human kind.

Finance and Speculation (EP) – Since banking had its 'big bang' moment in the early 80's, the financial industry has expanded well beyond itself. In the US for instance, banking creates 4% of jobs, represents 7% of the economy and yet takes 25% of all corporate profits. Research shows many industrial sectors are now following. Retailers, manufacturing, healthcare, all get five times the revenue from their financial operations from what they did in the 80s. [165] BP, the oil giant, made 25% of its profits from speculating. This money chasing money, is akin to a dog chasing its tail, simply moving money around in an exclusive circle, and thus detached from what is the real economy. NEL breaks this trend by ramping up competition on sustainability alone, nudging business to divest from finances and to power the…

The Green Revolution (EC) (CB) – By making VAT variable, it opens the floodgates for business to profit from the prevention of the planetary crisis. Currently, with next to no incentives, businesses are unable to design, plan and budget, excluding capitalists from cutting CO_2 emissions. Without such a policy, the 'green revolution' will likely remain a soundbite, nothing more.

Tax Avoidance (PC) – Is a subject that angers many. NEL turns the issue on its head by actively encouraging business to avoid tax. Secondly, by setting the axis on the median rate of sustainability for each particular industry, the treasury no longer has to foot the bill for cleaning up. Not only does this deliver justice for all, but for a business, rather than trying to cover up the issue of avoiding tax (for fear of being publicly scorned), they will be eager to brazenly advertise how much tax they save themselves and consumers, as they will be cheaper, greener and riddled with public good, helping to offset a further friction point…

Cognitive Dissonance (PC) – Is a form of psychological anxiety, where a person has two or more contradictory beliefs. Few would deny capitalism has delivered untold wealth and wellbeing. Yet capitalism unrestrained, grinds our future chances down, making it akin to pressing hard on the accelerator with one foot (the short-term) while slamming the brakes with the other (the long-term). NEL aims to do away with the brake pedal altogether, by converging profits with public good, through the medium of competition and tax. In any Neo-ECO-liberalist state, whatever the business or whoever the consumer, you will have a financial incentive to do your bit, enabling all of us to push in one direction, essentially tapping into both the pleasure and reality principle, creating greater...

Civic Engagement (PC) – NEL makes it fundamentally harder to cross the moral line. Today, even the most conscientious of directors finds it hard to not slip, given the intense pressure from competition with many businesses actively avoiding tax, why should you? NEL changes this on several levels. To start, with the government actively encouraging you to avoid VAT, it is one less line to cross. Secondly, with the tax dependent upon sustainability it creates another moral line making it harder still to cheat. Thirdly, with all transactions made digital, fraudulent activity can be traced back at any time via the public ledger, and financial penalties - or otherwise - applied.

The Disparity in Wealth (PC) (EC) – Today, the financial markets are four times the size of global GDP and rising. With this are global dividends[166] and the share buybacks. The latter is often financed by debt and was a process illegal not so long back. Despite this, from 2008 they totalled $4.5 trillion in the United States alone.[167] The gap in wealth is widening, not narrowing, as millionaires become billionaires, and the billionaires, demagogues, all of which pay a smaller percentage of tax than cleaners. Today, it is estimated the richest 1% have a combined wealth greater than the poorest 4.6 billion. According to Oxfam Intl, in 2020, just 2,153 individuals emitted *twice* the carbon of the worlds poorest

50%. Those few were the world's richest, all billionaires. By turning up competition on sustainability, it pushes businesses to invest, which in turn reinvigorates what is the real economy, creating jobs. Nudging business to move away from finance could not come at a better time given the traditional constraints of capitalism are disappearing.[168]

Short-Termism (EC) (CB) (PC) – This is a trend that began in the post-war period. Fresh from college, 'management experts' were enlisted by businesses as they had learnt to maximise profits in a quicker fashion than the traditional methods employed. They went about restructuring companies by making the likes of technicians, engineers and designers redundant, saving huge amounts in labour costs. Then instead of investing in improving, say a torch – making it more durable, efficient and bright – they showed how profits could be significantly improved by using cheaper batteries (or none), a weaker lens, and turn what money they saved into marketing the product heavily instead. This may not improve customer satisfaction or enhance the long-term image of the brand, but it will sell more and bring in outside investment, as shareholders will be getting their money back thick and fast. Not only did this reverse the slow rise in product improvement, but with everything being so cheap, greatly exacerbated the throwaway culture of today. NEL addresses this by directing businesses to follow either of the two paths in the circular economy, correcting this long trend in short-term strategies.

Employment (PC) (EC) – This is part of the number one issue for voters. With NEL, the lowering of VAT is strictly incumbent upon reducing pollution and waste (CB) *not human labour*, a factor that businesses have gravitated towards in their eternal quest to drive down costs. This is largely due to the rise of the informatics and robotics, as highlighted in Jeremy Rifkin's *Zero Marginal Cost.*

NEL shifts the focus into going green, boosting employment across the board, from the non-skilled to the highly technical

Growth (PC)(EC)(CB) – The nature of business is to seek higher profit and growth. Politicians, pursue the same, kowtowing to policies that increase GDP, as they perceive it as the bell-weather for everything in society.[169] Yet Finland has one of the best educational systems in the world, but has a GDP per capita 25% lower. While Costa-Ricans live longer than the average US citizen but earn just 20% of their salary. Many environmentalists campaign for an end to growth since we are depleting the earth's resources at a faster rate than we can replace. NEL synthesises these concerns through refined growth i.e., continuing growth but on a sustainable course until the point where climate change no longer poses any peril and companies merge or mimic with the natural energy lines in nature.

Planned Obsolescence (CB) (PC) – To design products to become unfunctional and/or fall apart in order that consumers consume yet more, whilst knowing the consequences of which, feeds the planetary crisis, is insanity. NEL aims to nudge business off this by having them adapt to a circular economy.

Patent System (PC) (EC) (CB) – Allowing business to create a monopoly slows progress, and to have progress choked at a time when we desperately need to move fast to further sustainability/efficiency in order to quell the menace of climate change, is the equivalent of putting a gun to our head and pulling the trigger. With NEL, it presents better ways to reward innovators, be they individuals or business, while not causing monopolies, by way of auctions and varying the tax rate and brand.

A Consumer Enlightenment (PC) – Whether we like it or not, day-by-day we slowly veer closer to becoming a market society as everything around us is beginning to get priced. Yet if we are a democracy, as we march down this road it is our every right to be informed of the power we wield, as we have seemed to forget that education is what makes society civil. But before we click to buy, we are not properly informed of what practices a business employs, but deceived. The eco-label answers this, giving greater power to the public's collective conscience, which in turn helps us to restore...

Trust (PC) – Our trust in politicians and corporations has now diminished to the point where democracy and capitalism - the double helix of what runs both society and the economy - are being questioned. With NEL it nudges businesses away from this 'growth for growth's sake' mentality that has been allowed to linger in boardrooms and shifts them into making goods and practices that sustainable, effectively changing the focus from ways to reduce labour and material costs, towards lowering their carbon footprint and ecological breakdown along where the supply chain is based, a concern that has been climbing up the political agenda and where it will remain and bloat, until environmental breakdown no longer presents a threat, or, the worst will happen.

SUMMATION

The question posed at the beginning of this book was: 'Why do we tread a path that leads towards climate breakdown and what is stopping us from turning – Democracy, Capitalism, or Ourselves?'

Having read thus far, I hope you will agree the fault lies not with any one of these, but all three. For each is bound to an archaic socio-economic system that businesses are at fault for over-exploiting, governments for not reforming and the public for permitting our real needs and values to be repressed.

At the heart of all this lies our common currency and the price. It's the value we perceive, the profit a business seeks and what government's tap in order to re-invest in policies that help steer society *as they see fit.* A price, in essence, is the synapse of our economy, and money the energy that powers it.

Today, every minute around the globe, millions of transactions take place as we opt to exchange our time, labour and skills for products we believe will enhance our life, promoted so often through advertising. Yet every one of these demands resources and energy to make. Those sneakers you wear will likely need leather, nylon, viscose, synthetic rubber, plastic, Chromium and dyes; and each of these materials in turn, requires further resources to manufacture. They need machinery to extract and process them; machinery to mould them into footwear and transport them, which in turn need yet more materials to make. Then there is the power needed to operate those machines and yet more materials to make the tools that service them; materials and machines to construct, run and maintain the building where the company is based, the vehicles to distribute the finished goods to the marketplace where they will be sold, not to mention the task of decommissioning and waste.

Yet when we purchase a product, too few pause to consider the effects such goods will have upon the natural world. Choices such as these are as ethically jarring as they are mundane for the person on the street, because the few that want to know, can't. And for those that believe it doesn't affect them, it will. For when transactions are performed every minute in their millions, they impact upon the climate, stability and security of our world, as they influence the weather, water and landscape around us; the air we breathe,[170] the food we eat and the life of all living things.

The pricing mechanism that runs our economy today, was devised yonder back, at a time when our numbers were small and the earth vast, unexplored, waiting to be exploited through our 'godly right' and ignorance. Today, we know different. Finite and fragile, a living oasis in the blackness of space. Yet, by our own volition, so long as we remain bound to prices that do not recognize Gaia, our home,[171] we are well on course to destroy it.

The mechanism does not penalise those companies that take more over less, and as such a business merely shrugs at our extinction. Yet rather than acknowledge this flaw and commit to correcting it, governments merely pass the buck, presuming we 'humans' to be as rational as Spock, omniscient beings aka, homo-economicus,[172] able to navigate our way through the myriad of market choices in our quest to make the right decision for us, society and the planet.

Furthermore, this misplaced faith is underlined by the long-held belief that a growing business is good for the economy, and a growing economy delivers greater riches and revenue for all, while ignoring the inexorable fact, that it's growth that's causing our homes to flood, our forests to burn and crops to wither and die. All of which places further strain upon the economy, as it requires ever-increasing resources to repair, causing insurance premiums, commodity prices and taxes all to rise.

This oversight is unquestionably caused by the environment not being factored into the price, resulting in the economy and the environment being approached in completely separate ways, running counter to one another. Which begs the question *why*, considering:

- *Both* are public concerns,

- And both can be dealt with by *any* business/consumer.

There is no reason therefore, why *both* cannot be dealt with by the market, providing the signals and incentives are realigned to factor this.

Money is not immutable, after all, but an institution oiled and maintained by the sovereignty to help measure, record and exchange what we *all* value. Yet while its form has changed over the centuries, from coins to paper to digital codes, the values that dictate it have not.

But ours have.

Today, it is impossible to ignore the news flash before us – heatwaves, crop failures, wildfires - and we know we have to act.

We understand too that we are not detached from nature, its master, as we once thought, but beholden to it.

And we also know that it is us, with our growing numbers and ceaseless appetite, that is fast gnawing away at both it, and the foundations of what we most enjoy – the liberties and comforts civilization gifts us.

As citizens, we acknowledge and accept all of this. But as consumers we don't. Skill, knowledge, labour and scarcity are factors that help form a price, not the environment. This dismissal of the crisis in financial terms causes businesses to opt for paths that don't mitigate, but exacerbate the crisis - marketing over green innovation; robotics over cutting waste - which is further entrenched by hard competition as businesses *fight for survival* and growth, making the market out of touch with the reality we face, *our survival as a species.*

Here's Hayek, one last time:

> *'In no system that could be rationally defended would the state just do nothing. An effective competitive system needs an intelligently designed and continuously adjusted legal framework as much as any other. Even the most essential prerequisite of its proper functioning, the prevention of fraud and deception (including exploitation of ignorance) provides a great and by no means yet fully accomplished object of legislative activity.'*

Today, the public officials and corporations that are actively pursuing policies designed to reduce carbon emissions, are minute compared to the vast majority who sit and idly watch as the affects and effects of climate breakdown grow more visible around us. Neo-ECO-liberalism is a call to arms, for it is not what we choose however, but what the price mechanism advocates - the very antithesis of what money is founded upon, *a collective belief,* not denialism. They want to fight, but can't. For we all value stability and peace, not storms and floods or forced migration - what's at stake effects every one of us. As such the onus is on our governments to redesign the financial payment system to distribute this workload responsibly and fairly. Despite this, decades have rolled by, followed by decades of inaction. We must change this and VAT perfectly placed perform this, with the help of digitalisation.

Uniquely and intrinsically placed, VAT represents a monetary value and a bond between businesses and consumers, executed at the point of exchange, but can be a preferable store of account and measurer of value *as society justly recognises*. Therefore, by making the rate of VAT dependent upon the sustainability of the practice and product, but commensurate to their peers, by ranking and displaying the rates accordingly, it can better mirror these values and gift capitalists the opportunity to profit from a whole new financial value in the market, and can tackle this crisis far more effectively than any government in office, providing the leagues and divisions are fairly placed and we move to digitalisation and local tax offices.

In less than a week from now, as I write, the heads of nearly every state will be descending on Glasgow for COP26. There, they will remain locked in deep discussion as they attempt to forge an agreement on how best to stop our environment becoming hostile towards us. I am confident they will make their pledges, as I am that they will try to follow-up on these. Yet I remain most resolute that if they turn and march in the direction of sustainability, industries and consumers will be marching to a different tune in another direction as they always have, thus leaving it for governments to clear up – we need financial carrots, not regulatory sticks.

In 2019, the UK government signed £1 trillion of taxpayer's money to help shift to a net zero economy. This is being mirrored in most developed nations.

Although a good thing in itself, this doesn't make it right

when there exist more efficient ways to achieve this that are both fairer and above all faster!

For instance, in continuing to have a fixed rate of VAT, it fails to apportion the responsibility justly, as it charges individuals and businesses no matter the waste, carbon or pollution they emit.

Secondly, *if and when* a government does act, money is only passed back, from treasury to industry, which takes the funds on an uncertain journey that consumes time - that we do not have – and by then, the pollution has already been emitted, where it will remain, hanging over us for centuries to come.

Thirdly, the paths government choose to achieve Net Zero are but a tiny number of the many, many solutions we can be employing to tackle the crisis.

Fourthly, every transaction undertaken will continue to make industries ignore their responsibility to deal with the crisis until a point where regulations are imposed *unfairly* from above, or when public demand is imposed commercially. Until either of these are enacted, industries will continue, as they always have, to leave the crisis for governments to clean-up, while they carry on taking the environment for granted.

Lastly, money first came about under the aegis of having a universal appeal, which it has since lost. The final straw of which was in 1971, when the US broke away from the Bretton Woods agreement, which pegged its currency to gold. After which, all the major currencies followed, dissolving any intrinsic value they had overnight. Today, local forms of currencies and cryptocurrencies are springing up, not just for criminal use or as get-rich-quick schemes, but people see the value seeping out of their communities through financial institutions rather than being recirculated back into the local economy. This trend exposes a loss of confidence and belief in the state, and as such, weakens its national currency and can lead to inflation.

Now look at it from the perspective of using a variable VAT rate pinned exclusively to its carbon footprint and ecological breakdown. Here, an altogether different world emerges.

For one, with the median rate being positioned in the centre of each industrial sector and size, it comes as no extra burden to the taxpayer, eradicating that £1 trillion bill (in the UK's case) and the hotchpotch of schemes that act like a sticky plaster over a gaping wound i.e., the fundamental flaw in the price.

Secondly, it *adds value* to money, reviving that universal appeal that money has lost. For when performing any transaction, you will be settling our debt not to government, but the environment – the opposite of cryptocurrencies that use vast amounts of energy to mine digital coins.

Thirdly, it directly deals with the cause of greenhouse emissions, saving substantial time and crucially avoiding the dialectical pendulum of the parliamentary process, which for all its intended good, has left a trail of failures in its wake.

Fourthly, it apportions the responsibility more fairly for consumers and businesses alike, reconnecting us through our values.

Lastly, the first duty of any government is to protect its people, for which we pay taxes, but will a bomber stand up to a hurricane, or a tank stop a flood? Climate change represents our greatest threat, and if governments were to make variable VAT a reality, it decentralises the crisis allowing us to attain a *critical mass*, transforming our boardrooms into war rooms against climate change while striving to answer the needs of consumers who will all be seeking to get more for the buck, while saving our planet. Therefore, if we continue along the course of neoliberalism, we must embrace its *No1* principle by throwing the crisis to the market, not pick and choose, and the most effective way to realise this is by locking the environment into the price, changing the very nature of money, as a source for the public good.

<u>NOTES</u>

1 www.lifeworth.com/deepadaptation.pdf
2 https://www.bbc.co.uk/news/science-environment-49689018
3 Or how carbon dioxide absorbs heat.
4 Nicholas Stern, referring to climate change, author of the Stern report.
5 The Intergovernmental Panel on Climate Change (IPCC) The United Nations body for assessing the science related to climate change.
6 Marx saw this as a primitive form of communism, where everyone worked together as a single unit.
7 By Assets
8 2006
9 Adam Smith, known by many as the father of modern capitalism.
10 Natwest, Scottish Widows, Tesco Bank, Standard life Aberdeen, to name a few.
11 The title of the parliamentary investigation into why HBOS collapsed. https://publications.parliament.uk/pa/jt201213/jtselect/jtpcbs/144/144.pdf
12 KPMG, Ernst & Young, PricewaterhouseCoopers and Deloitte – represent the biggest accountancy firms in the world. It was reported in 2011 that combined they audit 99% of the companies on the FTSE.
13 'Postcapitalism', Paul Mason
14 Brilliantly exposed through the likes of Luxleaks, along with the Panama, Pandora and Paradise papers.
15 A term used in economics where wealth 'trickles down' from the rich into the pockets of other members of society.
16 Bhutan and New Zealand are two exceptions, measuring 'well-being' through natural, financial, and human and social health.
17 National Health Service, the publicly funded healthcare system in the UK
18 John Ashworth, Shadow Health Secretary, 2021. Later revised to 3% (more a slap in the face)
19 FT. 21/11/17
20 https://www.execpay.org/news/walgreens-boots-alliance-inc-2020-compensation-529
21 https://researchbriefings.parliament.uk/ResearchBriefing/Summary/CBP-8227
22 Donald Trump, in Hilton Head, South Carolina, Dec. 30th 2015.
23 https://iopscience.iop.org/article/10.1088/1748-9326/ac2966
24 The utility regulator.

25 https://leftfootforward.org/2017/10/multinational-companies-are-using-this-loophole-to-avoid-millions-in-corporation-tax/

26 Before covid

27 Guardian 2/12/16

28 July 2019. https://www.carbonbrief.org/climate-change-made-europes-2019-record-heatwave-up-to-hundred-times-more-likely

29 https://www.bbc.co.uk/news/science-environment-58494641

30 https://www.thieme.com/resources/66-resources/resources-for-students/1014-what-can-a-person-survive-the-borders-of-the-human-body

31 European Academies Science Advisory Council.

32 https://www.bbc.co.uk/news/science-environment-49483580

33 https://phys.org/news/2017-10-three-quarters-total-insect-population-lost.html

34 Economist, March 2019.

35 https://portals.iucn.org/library/node/46254

36 https://www.resourcepanel.org/reports/global-resources-outlook

37 https://www.theworldcounts.com/challenges/planet-earth/state-of-the-planet/world-waste-facts/story

38 https://www.smh.com.au/politics/federal/australia-s-climbs-the-list-of-wildlife-extinction-hotspots-20210303-p577dy.html

39 Since the 50's - https://www.cell.com/one-earth/fulltext/S2590-3322(21)00474-7

40 http://www.fao.org/documents/card/en/c/cb4827en

41 'The Constant Economy,' Zac Goldsmith.

42 https://af.reuters.com/article/commoditiesNews/idAFL2N1XY0WI

43 https://www.theguardian.com/environment/2021/sep/06/climate-crisis-transatlantic-flight-global-economy-gdp

44 Rana Foroohar, in her book: 'Makers and Takers', and The Bertelsmann Foundation.

45 Harvard University survey 2016

46 www.statista.com/chart/10155/british-consumers-who-distrust-brands/

47 Edelman Trust Barometer 2020.

48 https://www.theguardian.com/environment/2021/nov/07/few-willing-to-change-lifestyle-climate-survey

49 The belief that the free market functions best with low government interference

50 Six hundred tickets have already been sold, each for between $200–250,000 on Virgin Galactic. Nov 6th 2020.

51 'Thinking Fast and Slow,' David Kahneman or 'Phishing for Phools' by G. A. Akerlof & R. J. Shiller, all Nobel laureates.

52 A term used in the 19th Century for the Victorian industrialists who were seen to contribute positively, as depicted by Ford Madox Brown in his painting 'Work.'

53 https://www.ncbi.nlm.nih.gov/pmc/articles/PMC7364393/

54 https://static1.squarespace.com/static/5ebd0080238e863d04911b51/t/5fbfcb1408845d09248d4e6e/1606404891491/Advertising's+role+in+climate+and+ecological+degradation.pdf

55 The Cayman Islands has over $500 billion under management, more than all of the New York banks combined. 'Reconnecting Taxation,' Mulgan, Robin Murray.
56 Note. The standard efficiency of fridges (the first product it subjected to the label) was G to A. But as competition pushed manufacturers to become more efficient, the ratings of efficiency increased to A+ before A++ to where it stood at A+++ before updating them yet again, reverting to the original signage. This shows what businesses can achieve if companies are forced to be more transparent.
57 It is now said BP earns 15% of its income speculating.
58 BBC Sounds, the life scientific, Brenda Boardman 21st Sept 2021.
59 https://ec.europa.eu/energy/news/report-eu-energy-efficiency-requirements-products-generate-financial-and-energy-savings_en
60 https://ec.europa.eu/energy/en/topics/energy-efficiency/energy-efficient-products
61 Some countries outside the EU have now adopted the label
62 Before Brexit
63 £8.91 in 2021
64 www.bbc.co.uk/news/business-44885983
www.mnn.com/natural-beauty-fashion/stories/burberry-burns-clothes-and-accessories-worth-millions
65 https://www.cnbc.com/2019/04/12/helium-shortage-is-hitting-balloons-and-scientific-research.html
66 https://physicstoday.scitation.org/do/10.1063/PT.6.2.20200605a/full/
67 The Hut Group. The Guardian Saturday 17th Nov 2012.
68 A term devised by Orwell, for organisations who don't like transparency.
69 www.theguardian.com/business/2015/dec/15/starbucks-pays-uk-corporation-tax-8-million-pounds. www.bbc.co.uk/news/uk-politics-23019514.
https://next.ft.com/content/1e092a96-a419-11e5-873f-68411a84f346
70 An excellent example of this is the attempted takeover of Unilever by Kraft/Heinz.
71 James Logan, boss of the US envelope Company, quoted in 'Beyond the Promised Land' by David F Noble
72 https://www.justsecurity.org/63673/climate-change-our-greatest-national-security-threat/ https://www.militarytimes.com/news/your-military/2019/01/18/dod-majority-of-mission-critical-bases-face-climate-change- threats/
73 https://almanac.upenn.edu/archive/v48/n28/AncientTaxes.html
74 www.ethicalconsumer.org/latestnews/entryid/870/public-eye-shame-awards.aspx
75 https://www.telegraph.co.uk/finance/newsbysector/banksandfinance/9641806/Occupy-protesters-were-right-says-Bank-of-England-official.html
76 www.taxresearch.org.uk/Blog/2015/11/12/crickhowel-is-not-good-protest-it-is-just-poor-television/
77 https://docs.google.com/spreadsheets/d/12Jdgaz_qGg5o0m_6NCU_L9otur2x1Y5NgbHL26c4rQM/edit#gid=1364122473

78 There is currently a mass techxodus, where tech companies are relocating from New York and San Francisco to Miami as it offers tax breaks, cheap loans and less regulation.

79 https://www.marketwatch.com/story/apple-benefited-from-145-billion-illegal-tax-break-eu-rules-2016-08-30

80 Even Her Majesty the Queen and Prime Minister of the UK, have jumped ship and joined those who pay little in the way of tax.
www.mirror.co.uk/news/world-news/queens-10m-tax-haven-scandal-11474055
www.independent.co.uk/news/uk/politics/what-difference-between-tax-avoidance-evasion-david-cameron-offshore-panama-papers-a6974791.html

81 Robert Dahl, On Democracy

82 A champion for Neoliberalism

83 www.bbc.co.uk/news/magazine-18624350

84 180,000 (as per parliament) members divided by 66 million (World bank) living in the UK.

85 Furthermore, the average age of members stood at 57. Hardly a representation of the populace.

86 Numbering 993,000 as of August 2019. RSPB have well over a million members.
https://researchbriefings.parliament.uk/ResearchBriefing/Summary/SN05125.

87 https://qz.com/899586/global-voter-turnout-is-dropping-dramatically-across-the-world/

88 https://freedomhouse.org/report/freedom-world/2021/democracy-under-siege

89 https://yougov.co.uk/topics/politics/articles-reports/2019/11/07/which-issues-will-decide-general-election

90 www.huffingtonpost.ca/entry/climate-change-canada-election-2019_ca_5d2cb2c6e4b08938b0990248

91 https://roymorgan.com/findings/7504-most-important-problems-australia-the-world-february-2018-201803051043

92 65% of US citizens think the government is doing too little.
https://pewresearch.org/science/2020/06/23/two-thirds-of-americans-think-government-should-do-more-on-climate/

93 https://www.bbc.co.uk/news/world-58549373

94 https://www.nobelprize.org/prizes/economic-sciences/1987/solow/lecture/

95 https://www.bbc.co.uk/news/business-46122407

96 More the opposite. One couple found no less than 700 faults with their new house.
https://www.pontefractandcastlefordexpress.co.uk/news/people/couple-discover-staggering-700-faults-with-their-brand-new-280-000-house-1-9632631

97 https://www.theguardian.com/business/2019/feb/26/persimmon-profits-help-to-buy-scheme

98 Based on a 3 bedroomed semi-detached house it would cost on average £10,000 to install a ground source heat pump, £9,000 to fully insulate, £6,000 for triple glazing, £6,000 to install solar panels and a grey water system £1,000.

[99] https://theconversation.com/the-uk-has-some-of-the-least-energy-efficient-housing-in-europe-heres-how-to-fix-this-151609

[100] https://www.essexlive.news/news/essex-news/insulate-britain-m25-protests-protestors-5925299

[101] You could argue there are more – to raise funding for example, but Occam's razor is best applied here.

[102] https://www.theguardian.com/politics/2021/sep/16/tax-lost-in-uk-amounts-to-35bn-almost-half-say-campaigners-due-to

[103] http://www.taxresearch.org.uk/Blog/

[104] The UK supermarket Tesco's has been derided for charging women considerably more for a razor over men, despite them costing the same to produce.

[105] https://www.statista.com/statistics/236943/global-advertising-spending/

[106] Sixty-nine percent of US citizens are "somewhat worried" or "very worried" about climate change. 2019 survey by Yale University. https://climatecommunication.yale.edu/wp-content/uploads/2019/01/Climate-Change-American-Mind-December-2018.pdf

[107] https://www.journal.chestnet.org/article/S0012-3692(18)32723-5/fulltext

[108] UN Intergovernmental Panel on Climate Change.

[109] https://www.ipcc.ch/sr15/

[110] https://www.uk.reuters.com/article/us-britain-starbucks-tax/special-report-how-starbucks-avoids-uk-taxes-idUSBRE89E0EX20121015

[111] The Constant Economy, Zac Goldsmith.

[112] Schumpeter describes creative destruction as the "process of industrial mutation that incessantly revolutionizes the economic structure from within, incessantly destroying the old one, incessantly creating a new one." ... Creative destruction theory treats economics as an organic and dynamic process. Investopedia Nov 2019

[113] The Indian currency rupees derives from rupa (head of cattle), while capital comes from the Latin word capita, meaning 'head'.

[114] Packs of mackerel have been used in prisons.

[115] Or as Stanley Jevons phrased it 'a double coincidence of wants.'

[116] Access to cash review, fairer finance research group

[117] UK Fina

[118] Arvidsson, Hedman and Segendorf 2018

[119] https://newsroom.barclays.com/r/3492/going_for_gold_-barclays_celebrates_50th_anniversary_of

[120] www.dutchnews.nl/news/2019/04/amsterdam-concerned-at-wave-of-atm-blasts-and-grenade-attacks/   www.bbc.co.uk/news/uk-northern-ireland-48063852

[121] Excluding gasoline

[122] www.imf.org/external/platopubs/ft/fandd/2018/06/pdf/fd0618.pdf

[123] https://www.pca.state.mn.us/green-chemistry/bpa-thermal-paper

[124] The Economist 3rd-9th Aug 2019

[125] www.ecb.europa.eu/paym/groups/pdf/cogeps/121022/A_11_ECB_Cost_of_payments_study.pdf?f952dbf6849bf1babce0df7c95711601

[126] Washington Post (Dec. 2014)

[127] This includes burglaries and larceny. www.fbi.gov/file-repository/bcs-annual-2011.pdf/view - I use these backdated figures, as any date forward of this, the FBI does not post the sums stolen.

[128] The area that goes unmonitored by the government and is regularly untaxed.

[129] https://en.wikipedia.org/wiki/Rent-seeking

[130] www.eesi.org/files/climate.pdf

[131] www.gov.uk/guidance/rates-of-vat-on-different-goods-and-services

[132] World Green Building Council.

[133] A passivhaus is a building designed and built to a rigorous energy efficient design, so they use next to no energy for heating or cooling, reducing their ecological footprint.

[134] See embodied energy on page....

[135] www.hsph.harvard.edu/epacenter/epa_center_99-05/research.html

[135] 'Energy Efficiency and the Demand for Energy Services' L.D. Danny Harvey.

[137] Its estimated size is 3.43 million km².

[138] Weiss et al 2006.

[139] www.bam.com/en/blog/case-study-sustainability-one-angel-square-manchester

[140] Ritchie, Hannah: Roser, Max 'Plastic Pollution' Our World in Data.

[141] https://bioresources.cnr.ncsu.edu/resources/the-effect-of-colorants-on-the-content-of-*heavy*-metals-in-recycled-corrugated-board-papers/

[142] https://www.royalholloway.ac.uk/research-and-teaching/departments-and-schools/biological-sciences/news/microplastics-impact-in-river-thames/

[143] https://en.wikipedia.org/wiki/Bisphenol_A

[144] www.breastcanceruk.org.uk/our-campaigns/no-more-bpa/

[145] https://www.theguardian.com/society/2021/mar/28/shanna-swan-fertility-*reproduction*-count-down

[146] https://ehp.niehs.nih.gov/doi/10.1289/ehp.0901200

[147] https://www.sciencedirect.com/science/article/pii/S0160412020322297

[148] Industrial ecology and sustainable engineering. T.E. Graedel. B.R. Allenby

[149] https://www.gov.uk/government/statistics/companies-register-activities-statistical-release-2020-to-2021/companies-register-activities-2020-to-2021

[150] https://www.ons.gov.uk/businessindustryandtrade/business/activitysizeandlocation/bulletins/ukbusinessactivitysizeandlocation/2019

[151] https://www.gov.uk/government/organisations/hm-revenue-customs/about/recruitment

[152] Combined, the leaked paperwork consisted of 25 million documents.

153 Over the next few years, HMRC will be reducing the number of offices. Of those surviving, they will be located in Glasgow, Edinburgh, Belfast, Newcastle, Leeds, Liverpool, Manchester, Nottingham, Birmingham, Bristol, Cardiff, Croydon and Stratford.

154 The Joy of Tax, Richard Murphy.

155 International chamber of shipping.

156 Joseph Stiglitz, Professor of economics and Nobel laureate.

157 These include France, Spain, Italy, Portugal, Cyprus, Malta, Slovenia and Croatia.

158 2012. International Maritime Organisation (IMO).

159 https://www.nature.com/articles/s41467-017-02774-9

160 It must be said however, that not all goods shipped long distances will be more environmentally damaging than those within the Nel state travelling smaller distances. But without regulatory assessments and monitors put in place, there exists no way of knowing.

161 Since writing this, the EU have proposed something similar called a carbon border tax, which it intends to impose on cement, steel. Aluminium & fertiliser, the connotations of which have yet to be seen.

162 https://ec.europa.eu/commission/presscorner/detail/en/qanda_21_3661

164 https://www.statista.com/statistics/236943/global-advertising-spending/

165 Rana Foroohar - as quoted on BBC Radio 4, The New Age of Capitalism.

166 Janus Henderson Dividend index

167 JPMorgan

168 *Consumer Choice* (now largely hoodwinked by the veil), *the state*, (no longer having quite the power to curb corporations due to globalisation & mulitnational institutions, lobbyists) and good *investigative journalism* (which is sadly disappearing thanks to the public switching to readily available and free news online).

169 www.youtube.com/watch?v=77IdKFqXbUY

170 https://www.bbc.co.uk/news/science-environment-58657224

171 Gaia, is the theory that the Earth is a living entity, greater than the sum of all the living and non-living aspects that make up the planet.

172 Homo economicus or economic man, is the depiction of humans as all rational and forward-thinking accumulator of goods.

Printed in Great Britain
by Amazon